Old Friends

Old Friends

A Collection

LEON HALE

WINEDALE PUBLISHING
Houston

All rights reserved under International and Pan-American
Copyright Conventions,
Published by Winedale Publishing Co., Houston
Distributed by the Texas A&M University Press Consortium

Library of Congress Cataloguing-in-Publication Data

Hale, Leon.
Old friends : a collection / Leon Hale.
p. cm.
Selected articles from the author's column in the Houston Chronicle.
Includes indexes.
ISBN 0-9752727-0-5 (alk. paper)
I. Title.
PN4874.H218A25 2004
814'.54--dc22

www.winedalebooks.com

Manufactured in the United States of America

2 4 6 8 9 7 5 3

Book Design by Harriet Correll

For B.

Contents

Introduction

A friend who is not a regular reader of my column in the *Houston Chronicle* once introduced me at a gathering by saying, "Everything this fellow writes goes into a book."

Let me tell you how far from correct that statement is. It's not only out of the ball park. It's not even close to the city where the ball park stands.

Between 1997 and 2003, I wrote more than a thousand columns for the *Chronicle*. Fewer than seventy of those pieces were chosen for this collection.

I did the choosing, along with my partner, Gabrielle Fraser Hale. We looked for pieces we thought might be of as much interest, forty or fifty years hence, as they are now. Few rose to meet that level.

For me, this sort of self-editing is a formidable and humbling chore. It reminds me of all the days I've spent at a keyboard producing stuff that's only pretty good, that starts out promising and stays on track two-thirds the way through—then sags and collapses and begs to be re-written before it deserves placement in a book. The columns in this collection have not been rewritten. They've been mildly edited to fit better into book format. Otherwise they appear as they did in the paper, written under deadline.

My well-meaning friend—up there in the first paragraph—was misled because he has read my stuff not in the paper but only in previous collections. There have been four of those, two of which are still in print. Their titles are *Home Spun* and *Easy Going*.

Five popular pieces from the out-of-print books are included in this collection, to prevent them from fading out of print forever. These elderly columns include "The Chamber of Commerce Bull," which many regular readers of the column call their all-time favorite. This piece and two others, the first three in Section 3, were originally reprinted in *A Smile From Katie Hattan*, my first collection. The last two columns in the book are from *Texas Chronicles*.

Readers of *Old Friends* who are not familiar with the *Chronicle* column may be puzzled by a couple of my eccentricities. My practice, for example, of referring to readers as customers. I've been doing that for forty years and evidently I'll not ever stop the habit. And then new customers sometimes wonder who I am talking about when I mention my partner, which I often do. She is my wife. And maybe I ought to go ahead and explain that Charlotte Brontë, in this book, is a Labrador retriever.

My thanks go to the *Houston Chronicle* for permission to reprint the columns that have run in that journal. Thanks also to my friend Sherry Adams, the *Chronicle's* editorial librarian, who somehow exhumed a thousand columns out of the paper's digital morgue, so this book could be created.

Leon Hale 2004

1.

Curb this Enthusiasm

Did I hear you say you're about to establish a compost pile in the back yard? Maybe you better talk to me first, as I have had valuable experience in this field.

Three years ago I decided we were wasting far too much organic material at our house so I got hold of some literature on composting and studied it and saw that making compost is a noble calling.

The wonderful thing about it is, you take all the vegetable matter you normally dump in the garbage grinder and you put it in your compost pile and stand back. Then here come these jillions of bacteria and they break down the stuff you have put in and convert it to compost which is beneficial to plants, and to Earth, and therefore to all of mankind. Isn't that exciting?

One writer of the compost literature called those bacteria "Mother Nature's tiny helpers." I liked that, and thought it was cute. (I don't think so now, but I did in the beginning.)

The same writer wrote that it is not necessary to buy a lot of expensive equipment, because you can do your composting in a pile in the corner of the yard or even in plastic garbage bags. But my feeling at the time was that any composting worth doing is worth doing well so I bought proper equipment.

At a store where such things are sold, a young fellow introduced me to a large compost bin. It looked like a dog house designed to accommodate a canine about the size of that Marmaduke creature in the comics.

I bought three of those. I've tried to forget what they cost but I think it was something like sixty bucks a copy.

Grass clippings off the lawn went in those bins. Weeds out of the flowerbeds. Trimmings off the shrubs. Leaves off the trees. Peelings off the potatoes.

Lettuce leaves wilted beyond use. Hulls off the peas. Leeks, lentils, and lima beans that didn't get eaten. Pumpkin, peppers and pintos—if they weren't consumed they went to the compost bins. Rinds off watermelon and cantaloupes. Anything forgotten and spoiled in the bottom of the refrigerator became treasure, to be converted to compost.

I was pleased to read in the instructions that the very cardboard cartons the bins came in could be composted, so I chopped them up and pitched them in and stirred.

At the grocery store I took up the habit of looking for compost fodder, such as bunches of carrots with beautiful green tops, inedible but compostable. That first spring I must have lugged home a bushel of roasting ears. An ear of corn is one hundred percent edible to a mule but to a human it's ninety percent throwaway, nothing but silk, shuck and cob, the perfect produce for a compost bin.

I bought an electric juicer and began squeezing orange juice every morning. Fresh-squeezed is good but also you have all that excellent waste, daily piles of orange peelings for your compost bins.

I discovered that such things as compost tools exist, and I bought them. One is a turner, a metal shaft with folded wings on its sharp bottom. You plunge that sucker down in your compost and when you pull up on it the wings unfold and tumble the material and aerate it so Mother Nature's tiny helpers can carry out their assignment.

Now, if you're ready, I'll tell you how much compost I have harvested in three years. None. That's how much.

Toward the end, before I quit, I could dig in those bins and find orange peelings and corn cobs, been in there two years and still looking exactly like orange peelings and corn cobs. I even found egg shells, intact as the day they were laid. I found little bits of the cardboard cartons I shredded the day I bought the bins.

I talked to people who know about composting. They said I didn't water my compost enough, or else I watered it too much. Or I failed to turn it often enough, or I turned it too much. Or I didn't add any fertilizer, or I added too much.

To solve this problem, whatever it might have been, I went out on the edge of town and found a place where they sold me a pickup load of the nicest compost for about twenty-five bucks. The three bins I am using to store fireplace wood.   ∾

Flying Fish

$\mathcal{B}$ack home from a long weekend of fishing out in the Texas Hill Country.

Before I left Houston one of the customers told me to bring back a fish story, and I certainly intended to do that. However, I sure didn't expect to experience what I'm about to tell you. I wonder if any other fisherman ever has.

First a little background.

Every year at this season I go with a small bunch of guys out in the Llano River country and we camp a few nights, and fish, and cook, and at night around the fire we talk mostly about what we did on previous trips. We've been doing this now for twenty-odd years.

We camp on the James River, a short clear stream with a rocky and gravel bottom and frequent stretches of bubbly rapids feeding into quiet pools. Just a sweetheart of a place to loaf.

That country is loaded with wildlife. Deer, turkey, huge jackrabbits, and birds of a hundred kinds. One of the birds we like to watch for is the osprey. We always see them in flight and hope to be watching when one dives for a fish.

The osprey is a spectacular fisherbird. It dives with great speed and often from tall heights and it hits the water feet first and grabs its prey in its talons and flies off. When it splashes down, sometimes the sound is like a shotgun firing.

OK, so I'm fishing about half a mile upstream from the camp, using a flyrod. I'm a long walk from being a proficient flyrodder. I've owned a rod for several years and without fail I use it once annually, on this Hill Country trip. Mainly what I do out there is practice casting, and after three days I've usually remembered how to cast as well as I did when we left the river the year before. I'm always amazed when I hook a fish.

So I'm wading about knee deep, and I've caught a couple of bream that were fun on the light tackle, and I'm not really thinking about catching anything bigger. I've tied on a little yellow bug, with red and white rubbery legs. That's what I caught the bream on. But then I hook this bass.

To a real bass fisherman it's a small bass. It jumps once and I think back now and I'm guessing it's two pounds. Two pounds of bass on a light flyrod is a lot of action to me. My old ticker is banging away when that fish bends the rod and makes that silvery leap.

Then this extraordinary event comes to pass. An osprey dives out of the sky and—ka-POW—it hits the water and grabs my bass with both feet and starts flying off.

I'm so startled I almost drop the rod when it begins moving in my hands. It's moving because that hook is still in the mouth of the bass and the leader is still tied to the hook and so now what I've got on the end of my rig is not just a bass but an adult osprey in addition, and it's flying away and taking line off my reel.

I get the rod tip up and haul back. I figure the hook will pull loose, or else that bird will feel the pressure and let go of the bass.

Neither thing happens. The hook is apparently buried deep in the fish's mouth and the osprey is not about to give up its prize even though I hooked the bass first and feel it's mine by rights.

This is a big bird. Wing span probably close to six feet. It circles over the river a time or two and gives me a little slack and I pump and reel frantically but it's no use.

Carrying both my fish and my flyline, the osprey turns on the gas and goes straight upstream, gaining speed and altitude, stripping line from my reel and all I can do is just stand there and hold on and see what happens.

When the line finally went slack I stepped it off along the bank. That bird took ninety feet of flyline off my reel, plus nine feet of leader and almost another 120 feet of backing. Got my fish, too, and also my little yellow bug with the white rubbery legs.

Back at camp, during happy hour, I told the gang my story but not one of them believed a word of it.

(Author's note: However, I did have a lot of fun out of this story after it appeared in the paper. The best thing that happened, I got a letter from a fellow who said he was driving on Ranch Road 1871 near Mason, a few miles from where we camp, when a two-pound bass fell out of the sky and splattered against his windshield.) ∽

A Suspicious Mind

A certain company I do business with wants to give me a present. Several presents, in fact.

It has written me a nice letter about this. The letter shows pictures of the presents and they're pretty nice. I wouldn't mind having them.

The letters say I would receive these gifts simply because the company appreciates my business. It asks nothing in return. No obligation whatsoever. Nothing to buy.

It says I can have three or four presents if I want them. Even more. I can have up to three each of three different gifts pictured. That means I could get a total of nine of these gifts. Listen, that would shorten my Christmas shopping list significantly because the company says the stuff will come to me "individually boxed and attractively gift wrapped."

So I am tempted.

But I'm also suspicious. I turn the letter over and look down at the bottom where I expect to see the catch. Do I have to subscribe to a magazine that I don't want? Must I sign up for a credit card with an introductory interest rate of 3.9%, but probably rises to eighteen percent after two months?

I find no such thing. The letter reassures me. It says there is no hidden catch.

Isn't that nice? I've been wanting to hear that from a lot of companies for many years.

The nearest to a catch I find is that I must pay $3.95 in shipping and handling charges. For each gift item. Which means that if I accept nine of the gifts, they will cost me $35.55.

Should that bother me at all? If you are going to present me with a nice gift, the least I can do is pay for its handling and shipping.

And yet it does bother me a little. I mean it takes something away from the gesture. It reminds me of the time the fellow called and offered me a mess of turnip greens, and all I had to do was drive fifteen miles to get the greens which I can buy for six bits at the grocery store down the street.

Which is not exactly the same thing as the company's gift offer but it's related. It's not the same species but it's in the same genus.

Something else I have to do to receive the gifts is fill out a form showing my name and mailing address. Something about that causes me to wonder.

This company already has my name and address. It's on the envelope containing the offer of the gifts, and it's exactly right, zip code and all. So why does the company ask me to fill out a form?

If it really wants to give me a present, why not just send it on to the address that's already in the files?

This causes me to think of how many times in my life I have filled out address forms, and the total must run into the hundreds. It's my feeling that most of those times, filling out forms has not resulted in anything that pleased me. Therefore I have developed an aversion to filling out forms.

So you now see what I have decided.

My decision is, no thanks. I don't want those gifts because I am suspicious of the company's motive. I don't know exactly what its motive is but somehow I feel that in the home stretch the benefit will be to somebody other than me.

And I feel somewhat sad that things have come to this, that I can't accept a gift from a firm because I figure it is somehow conning me. I don't find anything in this letter to suggest that and yet I can't escape the feeling.

That feeling has been hammered into me over the years by scores and scores of other letters offering me what appeared to be most generous propositions and yet they turned out to be just sales gimmicks and not to my benefit in any way.

It's sad because this firm offering me the gifts may not have any hidden motive at all, and I have become so suspicious of gift offers that I'm unable to receive one with grace.

Let's say I get a letter like this:

"Dear Sir: You have been selected randomly from our customer base to receive a $100 bill, as an expression of our appreciation for your business. Absolutely no strings attached. All you have to do is fill out the enclosed form, return it in our self-addressed envelope, and we'll send you the money."

You think I'd respond to that? I would not. That's how suspicious I've become.   ∾

He's Got Experience

*T*his is for men only. In fact, it's only for young men who are about to get married, or who haven't been married very long.

You need advice. You don't think you do, but you're wrong.

I am here to help you. I'll give you a few pieces of advice which, if followed, will make your marriage go more smoothly. I learned all these the hard way, through more than forty years of married life.

1) First, don't marry a stranger. My experience says that the foremost of all marital problems is the result of couples getting married when they don't really know one another. If you've already married a stranger, I'm not saying you can't have a good life together but sometimes you'll have to work pretty hard at it. See the seven items below.

2) Every wife needs to be hugged at least once a day, and twice is better.

The importance of a hug cannot be overemphasized. But I don't mean one of these quick hugs like you'd give your sister. A hug like that, where you sort of glance off one another, is all right for relatives and friends but for married couples it doesn't mean any more than saying, "Have a nice day."

Good hugging takes practice. It mustn't be hurried. I would say thirty seconds is a minimum hug time. A full minute is not too long. I'm convinced that a lot of couples have been quick-hugging for years without understanding the value of a true hug.

What you have to do is stay hugged long enough for the warmth and the tingling to start passing back and forth between you. A mysterious mutual restoration takes place here. If you've not experienced that, you haven't learned to hug yet.

Don't let go until you've felt the feeling. If she tries to let go too soon tell her, "Wait, I'm not through yet." She'll understand.

3) Next to strangers marrying, the biggest problem is financial. If you don't have enough money to pay the rent and medical bills and buy groceries and go out to a Mexican restaurant once a week, you've got a recipe for marriage trouble.

The solution to this—other than somehow suddenly getting rich—is to share information. Don't keep money secrets from her. I've known husbands who've gone to the brink of bankruptcy while their wives thought everything in the money department was perfectly cool. Show her the numbers. Tell her, "Look, honey, this is how it is. Our bank balance is $23.16."

4) One of these times you'll come home and find her crying in the kitchen. Only thing to do is hold on to her and let her get it done. You can ask what's the matter but probably she won't tell you, if in fact she knows.

Women simply need to cry now and then. I think it's a way they release stress. Men ought to do it too but most of us think it's a show of weakness and so we stuff it. I think that's why women live longer. When she cries, see Numbers 2 and 5.

5) This is an old one but it's still solid. Every day, tell her you love her. You can demonstrate forty ways that you do, by bringing in gifts and all the other ways. But she needs to hear it, man.

15

However, don't over-do. I mean don't say, "Please pass the potatoes and I love you." Pick your times.

Many guys are not comfortable about saying, "I love you." I recommend practice. Go out in a park or in the country and find a cow or a tree or a blooming plant and tell it, "I love you. I love you. I love you."

Pretty soon that short declarative sentence becomes easier to get out. You need to do this.

6) Don't let insignificant situations cause trouble. If a secretary at the office borrows your handkerchief and leaves lipstick on it, throw it away. Lipstick on handkerchiefs, taken home, can lead to divorces.

7) Don't be shy about buying flowers to take home. Other guys may grin at you when you walk out but the women will envy your wife.

8) Sex? I knew you'd ask about that. I'll say this much: There'll be times when she'll say she doesn't feel like it. Be patient. There'll be times when you don't feel like it, either. Trust me.   ∾

Country-Style Rapture

For me, Christmas is already here. I'm on the front porch of the old country house in Washington County. The weather is sunshiny perfect, and there's no place I'd rather be.

I don't need anything beyond what I can reach from this old rocking chair I'm in. Don't want a present. Don't need any turkey or pumpkin pie or parties with eggnog. Just let me sit here and bake in the warm sunshine.

I've got my bum leg propped up on a cardboard box and my britches pulled up so the sun can heat the rheumatism in my sore knee and I can feel the healing going on in that creaky joint. Give me enough time here on the front porch and I may yet be able to dance on New Year's Eve.

What's happened to me is, I've entered into a sort of country-style rapture. In my experience, these events are rare.

Beneficiaries of such a condition forget any troubles they've been facing. If they've had physical discomfort (such as bad knees), the discom-

17

fort goes away. If they have financial trouble, they can't remember what such troubles were. Family problems? Forget about them.

What brings about this beautiful mind state? I wish I knew. It's not chemical. I haven't had as much as a weak beer, and I don't pop pills. This is just something that happens.

It has happened to me rarely. Maybe six times in all my years.

I once thought the first time was when I was on assignment down in Mexico City in the '50s. I'd been down there maybe two weeks. Things hadn't been going so well. Working in a country where you can't handle the language can be frustrating.

One afternoon I'd had an appointment with a person who'd promised to help me and we didn't hook up, probably because I'd misunderstood the where or the when. Walking back to my hotel, I was beginning to feel as if that trip to Mexico was a waste of time and expense.

I came to a little restaurant with tables outside. I took a seat there, in the sunshine. The weather was similar to what we're having here now. Calm. Mild.

The waiter took a long time coming, and I didn't care. It was siesta hour, and an almost unnatural quiet settled over that neighborhood, in one of the largest and busiest cities of the world.

Gradually a most extraordinary and pleasant relaxation came to me. Spoke to me, saying, "Hey, relax. All that stuff you're trying to get done isn't so important. You're not going to change the world."

And then from across the street somebody who was passing up the siesta began stroking a guitar, calm and slow, and it was beautiful, and for a few minutes I felt so fine.

Years later when I was back down in Mexico I tried to describe that experience to a guide who was helping me and he smiled and said, "Señor, you were feeling for a little while what it means to be a Mexican."

Later on I came to realize that I'd had that feeling before. When I wasn't anything but a shirttail kid one day I dug some worms and went to the creek to fish. Nobody with me except my old dog Jiggs.

We stopped at a hole we knew at a bend in the creek and cut a willow pole and baited a hook and the day was perfect, warm and calm. I lay back on the bank, in the sun, and that incredible feeling of well-being came to me.

It spoke of how fine it was to be alive, and comfortable, and unafraid. And about the importance of whether I caught a fish or not. Fishing had little importance, and wasn't why I was there on creek with my dog.

Probably psychiatrists and psychologists, and other experts in how the mind works, will have a name for this condition. I don't know what to call it.

I've experienced it, most times, in places where I love to be. On a river out in the Hill Country, for example, when I'm with friends and we're just lying around in the sun, with nothing important to do any time soon.

Maybe it has something to do with sunshine. Because clouds have moved in since I began this, here on the front porch, and the feeling has left me.   ❧

Togetherness

My Friend Mel came by the house the other morning, earlier than normal, before I'd had my second cup. He said:

"Hey, you look like you're feeling a little pale. Are you sick?"

Told him no, I was just a couple of hours short on sleep. The night before my partner and I had been to a party where the dancing lasted past my bedtime.

"Dancing?" He seemed amazed. "You actually go dancing?"

Sure, every chance I get if the music's not too fast. I love dancing.

"But aren't you getting, you know, a little long in the tooth for that kind of thing?"

Told him I wasn't aware of an age limit on dancing. Anybody who can still walk can still dance, if they have the right music. And it's good exercise.

He was shaking his head and grinning. "I've just never understood why so many people are nuts about dancing. I can't see the point of it.

Christina (his ever-loving wife) used to be crazy about dancing, when we first met. But I couldn't dance and didn't want to learn. I doubt she's ever forgiven me for that. Still brings it up once in a while, after forty-six years."

He ought to bring her over, I said. We'd put on a CD and I'd waltz her around the room a few times. Might do her good.

"She's probably forgotten how by now," he said.

Not possible. Nobody ever forgets how to swim, ride a bicycle, milk a cow, or dance.

"I don't see how it could do her any good. If she wants to dance she could do it at home by herself. We've got eight rooms and a hundred feet of hall she could dance in."

Told him that wasn't good enough. It needs to be done with another person. There's something mysterious and uplifting about moving together, taking the same steps, making the same turns, responding in the same way to the beat of the music.

"Makes no sense to me," Mel said. "It seems sort of silly."

Then think of yourself as an observer, watching a person dance, alone, on a stage. Say the person isn't even a very good dancer, so you're not entertained. But then a second person comes on stage and stands beside the first dancer and they begin to dance together. Not touching, but making the very same moves, just perfectly, and in an instant they become interesting to watch. They create a togetherness that's worth watching, and even more fun to experience, with another person. It's almost a way of two people becoming one person.

"My Lord," Mel said, "you make it sound like sex."

Well, maybe it's kin to sex. It works in a lot of different activities. Reciting poetry, say.

"Poetry?"

Sure. The best teacher I ever had was back in high school. She was always making us memorize poems, and get up in front of the room and recite. Sometimes she'd put two students up there at once, both of them especially good at recitation, and they'd speak the verses together, the same pacing, the same expression. It was astonishing how entertaining, how much more interesting the poetry became, than when one person was reciting.

"My brother and I, doing carpenter work, used to drive nails together that way," Mel said. "We liked the sound of it, the hammers hitting the nails at the same time."

There you go, same thing. I think wild creatures enjoy this togetherness, too. Birds, especially.

"Come on, birds dancing?"

Well, sometimes they do, in mating rituals, but I was thinking more about their flying. Out in the Hill Country recently on a fishing trip, I spent a while in the company of a little flock of shore birds. They weren't familiar to me, and I'm not sure I found them in the bird book. Long bills and long legs. But the finest fliers. They played with me for half an hour. There were eighteen in the flock and they flew in the most beautiful and precise formation, and fast, too. They'd turn and dip and climb and land and take off all together, as one bird, and it was nice to watch.

I'm told birds fly in formation that way as protection from predators, but these whatever-they-were seemed to be doing it for fun.

The way people do on the dance floor, sometimes hours past their bedtime. ∾

Homework

One of the customers wrote me a letter about working at home, rather than going to an office. He asked for advice.

I've never felt comfortable about telling people what to do, but I've had enough experience at home office work that I think I can address this subject with confidence.

The last time I reported to an office to do a day's work was in 1956. Since then, I've worked at home and sent to the office what I produce.

In that time I helped raise two kids, from birth to college and marriage and grandchildren. Also I was the father-figure to seven dogs, counting the one I'm helping raise now, and a furry multitude of cats my kids used to bring home. I feel like a veteran home office worker.

This father who wrote for advice sounds like a nice person. Many women might fall in love with him just by reading his letter.

He is thirty. He and his wife have two pre-school children. His employer has offered him the option of staying home and doing his work on computer. He is trying to decide whether to do that, or stay in the car pool and keep on commuting.

He likes helping with the kids. He wants to spend what he calls quality years with them. His wife works part time, eight to noon, and loves her job. They are paying a person to come mornings and watch after the babies. The cost of that child care is high, and the child-care woman is about to quit, anyway.

So the father says he could work at home, and his wife could keep her job, and they could get by without the nanny. He asks what I think of that.

I think it's about as risky as going over Niagara Falls in a bad barrel.

Based on my own experience, I would say that plan might work if the father is prepared to endure some memorable mornings that will test his sanity.

There'll be times like this:

The mother is driving off to work at 7:30 and both babies are screaming because they don't want her to go. They don't quit yelling until around eight o'clock. Half an hour of baby-crying prepares the father to start his day's work feeling tired already.

His work of the day is special, assigned by the big boss, and he must have it done by 2 P.M. Nothing can interfere or else he'll never meet the deadline.

So at 9:15, his five-year-old comes in and announces that the toilet in the back bathroom is running over. He stops work and devotes half an hour to solving a plumbing problem, caused by his three-year-old daughter who has flushed a rag doll down the commode.

Back to work, then, until ten o'clock when both children come running to his desk to say that the dog has messed on the living room rug, and the cat is up the oak tree in the back yard and doesn't know how to get down. There goes another twenty minutes of work time.

At 10:30 one of the neighbor ladies comes over and brings a plate of brownies and talks ten minutes about how wonderful it is that there are husbands in this world who will stay home and watch after little children.

24

At eleven o'clock the three-year-old comes wobbling up to his desk and says she is sick and then proves it by vomiting brownies on his shoes.

His wife calls at 11:30 to say her boss wants her to work until three o'clock and is that all right? He says yes, but it takes all his resolve to get it out.

The doorbell rings and it's UPS with a package, and when the father opens the door the dog gets out and runs into the street while the children scream that he'll be killed, he'll be killed by a car. Getting the dog back takes until noon and by then it's time for lunch and when he sets it out for the children the little one develops diarrhea.

All I'm saying here is that if a young father decides to work at home and have quality years with his children, he needs to understand that there'll be days like that.

After forty-five years of working at home I've thought it might be nice to leave the house at seven o'clock and go to an office and come home about six and say to my wife, "Did anything happen today, honey?" ❧

Not Very High

*S*everal of the customers have been asking about Old Friend Morgan, so I drove down to the little Brazoria County town of Sweeny to check up on him.

O.F. has gained a considerable following over the last twenty years due to his part in our annual trip south to meet spring. Every March, we journey south to find spring, just to be sure it's coming. That trip was O.F.'s idea to begin with, and it has proved to be the most popular recurring topic in the history of this column.

O.F. has been down in the quilts now for way too long. I found him in a nursing home there in Sweeny. "I'm still kickin'," he said, "but not very high."

They've got him hooked up to various sorts of apparatus. Wires and tubes running out from under his covers. He didn't seem to be hurting much, although I didn't ask. If I had asked, he would have said no, whether he was hurting or not.

He hasn't quit. He's still figuring on getting out of there and walking away, and I wouldn't bet against it.

I almost laughed, thinking back to World War II when the U.S. Army handed O.F. a medical discharge and told him he had a bad heart and might not last a dozen years. He's eighty-three now.

From the neck down he seems pretty well worn out, but there's nothing wrong with his head. Voice still strong and clear. He's always talked big. I expect half the people in the nursing home can hear him.

Long ago, I used to watch my father meet up with one of his old buddies and I thought it was strange the way they visited. They'd take turns telling each other stories about their past, stories that both were familiar with and yet they kept telling them, just as if they could make them happen again.

And there in the nursing home, O.F. and I were doing that same thing.

I expect we've talked a hundred other times about the day in Mexico City that I was about to collapse on the streets from altitude sickness. That had to be in the early '60s.

So I was hanging onto a lamppost like a drunk, wondering if I was about to die, grieving that I didn't have a friend within a thousand miles. And who comes striding across Reforma Avenue but O.F. himself, and calls my name.

I had no hint he was anywhere in the hemisphere, but there he was, and he got me straightened out and helped me do my work. Morgan finding me that day, among those millions of strangers, you've almost got to figure that was somehow Planned.

So in the nursing home we told that story again and nodded, and approved it, and then moved on out to the Trans Pecos and relived the times we had out there. For years O.F. ran a mining operation for Dow Chemical in that rugged country of Coahuila state, across the Rio Grande from Big Bend National Park.

I used to visit him, and our friend Ray Labeff would fly down from Alpine in his four-seater and we'd go way deep into Coahuila, snaking

27

around the mountain peaks to land at huge ranches where O.F. was known. Wonderful adventures.

Just taking off and landing there at O.F.'s place was a hairy adventure to me. The strip climbed the side of a mountain and you landed uphill and took off downhill, no matter what the wind direction was.

We reviewed one of my favorites of all the stories I got out of those trips. This was the scotch raffle.

Now and then O.F. would raffle off a bottle of scotch there at La Linda, where he lived on the border just downstream from Big Bend. Among the mine workers and the cowboys off nearby ranches, a bottle of scotch was a great treasure, and all hands would take part in this raffle.

The procedure followed was not standard. The first name pulled out of the hat did not determine the winner. Instead, that name was eliminated, and so was the second, and so on and on. Until finally only two men remained, whose names had not been called. And there was much excitement, and even side betting on who would win the scotch.

The winner, then, was the one whose name was never called.

At the nursing home we dealt with these old stories until I thought O.F. was growing tired, so I left. I don't know if my visit helped him. But it helped me.   ~

The Corporal's Kindness

The reason I remember Memorial Day of 1943 is that it was my twenty-second birthday and I was a buck private in the Army, at Sheppard Field just outside Wichita Falls.

That night I lay in a GI bunk and listened to the eighteen-year-old kid cry into his pillow, and in the dim light I could see Corporal Gonzales squatting by the boy's bunk and hear him speaking soft words of comfort.

I had heard the boy cry before. He was in misery with his homesickness. But that was not so rare a condition.

What surprised me about that scene in the night was the kindness and understanding that Corporal Gonzales showed toward that suffering boy.

Corporal Gonzales was in the Army by choice. He was in it before Pearl Harbor, and he loved military life. It suited him perfectly. He had been placed in charge of a flock of us who had just been inducted.

He was short, chesty, strong, with the smoothest skin and the whitest teeth and eyes dark and yet brilliant. I want to say he walked erect but that doesn't tell you enough. He walked as if he were trying to stretch himself upward, to become taller.

Corporal Gonzales didn't need to be taller. He was a towering presence among us.

He made little speeches about how to get along in the Army. "Look, it's so easy. All you have to remember is, do as you're told, and if nobody tells you what to do, use your best judgment."

He always looked ready for inspection. His shoes glistened. His khakis were washed and bleached close to white, almost beyond uniform regulations. The creases in his pants were knife sharp.

His bunk was in the little room at the end of the GI barracks and it never looked slept in. When he rose from it he made it up immediately, with the top blanket stretched neat and tight so a quarter dropped on it would bounce. That was the test at inspection.

Corporal Gonzales was happiest when he was giving us close order drill while we marched. I can hear him singing out those orders, which were supposed to be in English but all drill instructors made a foreign tongue of them:

"Rye-flang, haw. Reep, haw. Reep, haw. Chir-up, hup, hoo, hut. Dresser up! Dresser up! Chir-up, hup, hoo, hut. Leff-oh-bligh, haw. Hut, hut. Ford? Haw. Chir-up, hup, hoo, hut. Dee-tail-l-l-l, haw!"

On the bus, when we were still in civilian clothes and approaching the gates of Sheppard for the first time, I noticed the boy and saw his pain and I knew he was in for a hard time.

His face was numb. His forehead creased. He was small, and a little overweight, and soft looking. Some kids at eighteen are simply not ready to leave home, and especially not to go into an Army and be trained to kill.

Tens of thousands of guys, most of them grandfathers now, remember the experience of walking out of civilian life and through the gates of a military installation and hearing the greeting of the thousands that had taken the same walk a short time before.

"Go back! Go back!" Waving their arms, trying to maintain serious facial expressions. Then singing, "You'll be saw-ree! You'll be saw-r-e-e-e-e!"

Most of us recognized that sort of taunt as GI humor, but to kids like the eighteen-year-old it had to be cruel torture. He already wanted to go back. He was already sorry.

For a while he was in my bunch, in the training, and he got through it with such suffering. Not just the physical stuff but the idea of it all, training to go into a war and kill people. For that kid it had to be unthinkable.

There must have been lots of them like that. I knew a few others before WWII was over.

In these days when we dwell on wars and deaths in wars, I keep returning to that scene where Corporal Gonzales bends over the crying boy and tries to comfort him. Maybe he was thinking this: Here's a boy crying for his mother, and within a year he may be overseas and in the middle of combat.

Wars have always been strange to me, and the longer I live the stranger they seem.   ∾

Pickup Snobbery

Probably you've noticed that people are often judged by the vehicles they drive. I was reminded of this recently when I attended a reunion in my old hometown.

A good many of the guys who came out of high school in that little town have apparently done very well indeed, and some don't mind showing that this is true. One way they show it is to return driving fancy wheels.

At the various gatherings held at reunions of this kind, car talk is common. Guys stand in little bunches and gossip about who came back driving a BMW, or a Mercedes, or one of those $60,000 Range Rovers.

"Old Bob must be doin' all right. Did you see what he's drivin'?"

Maybe Old Bob would be driving a Lincoln Town Car with a TV screen mounted just behind the driver's seat, for the entertainment of back-seat passengers. Or maybe one of those low-slung, Italian-made, look-at-me cars that cost half the mint in Denver.

I've always suspected some of those guys rent fancy cars when they go back to the old hometown. In fact, I threatened to do that myself, for this year's reunion.

My plan was to rent a limousine about half a block long, with dark windows, and roll up to reunion headquarters and sit a while in the back, until I was sure everybody was watching to see who would get out. At a pre-arranged signal I would have the chauffeur emerge and open the door for me, and bow.

However, I checked on the cost and decided I'd better not attempt that little scam.

What I started out to tell you is that it doesn't elevate my image when I return to the old hometown driving a white Ford pickup that's manually operated. I mean you have to crank the windows up and down.

Of all the vehicles I ever drove, this pickup is my favorite, not counting the '52 Merc I kept for twenty years when my kids were growing up. And yet, I have discovered that in certain social circumstances my truck is not considered proper.

At nice restaurants where they have valet parking, I've noticed that the parkers always put my pickup way in the back, apart from the nice shiny cars.

One time I had to go to the River Oaks Country Club to attend a meeting where I was to give a talk, and after the meeting I thought I would never get my truck back. The valet parkers must have put it down in the garage where they keep the machines used to maintain the greens and fairways.

In the summer when my partner and I go to Santa Fe, N.M., on vacation, we stay in one of these gated developments where security guys guard the entrance.

In July of this year a security person rang our bell and said we would have to move the pickup, which was parked in front of our door. It seems that the sight of that truck sitting in the sunshine was offensive to one of our neighbors, and that community has a rule that if the sight of anything offends anybody, it has to be gotten rid of.

That hurt my feelings because my pickup had just been washed, and was looking especially beautiful with its silvery toolbox gleaming just behind the cab, and yet there it was being offensive to the neighbors.

So I had to move the sweet thing down into an ordinary parking lot where the hired help kept their cars. I could not find out which neighbors did the complaining.

There was to be, about that time, a meeting of all the people who lived or stayed in the development, and I planned to get up at that affair and make a brief speech.

I rehearsed it several times until I had it down pat. Here is how it went:

"I rise in this meeting to apologize for offending the tender sensibilities of my neighbors by having a pickup truck parked in front of my door. The reason I drive this truck is that it's my only vehicle, and I make a living out of it. What I do is light hauling and yard work. I'm on vacation now but I wouldn't mind taking on a job or two to help pay the rent, which I consider to be pretty steep around here."

I thought it was a nice little speech but I didn't deliver it because my partner said if I did, she would leave me. ∾

Bread, Ball and Bananas

*F*ather's Day, and I'm thinking about the time my Dad took an entire stalk of bananas to a family reunion held on Grandma Hale's farm.

He loved to pull hot-dog stunts like that. When I was in overalls and $2 tennis shoes and following him around I admired that man fiercely, and thought he was the world's most outstanding father. However, I expect he was considered a show-boat type, especially by other men who would never think of taking a stalk of bananas to a reunion.

He hung the bananas on Grandma's front porch and left his open pocketknife on the railing so when the kinfolks arrived they could cut off bananas for themselves. Bananas were not common then and were counted a great treat in the country.

My father would sit on the porch and pretend to be interested in something else but he was listening for the exclamations of the new arrivals. "My stars, where in the world did all those bananas come from?" So then one of the women would explain that my father had brought them, and that's what he was looking for, his reward, his credit, for doing an extraordinary thing.

Another of his triumphs was sliced bread, at the same sort of gathering on the farm. He brought several loaves of sliced bread from a bakery in Fort Worth and this was at a time when our country relatives had never seen sliced bread and it generated more amazement even than the bananas.

It was like he had invented sliced bread, and I know it was a strain for him to keep from strutting around the front yard, so proud to be receiving all that praise.

Which came from the women, always, never the men. I suspect the men considered him a pain.

He was a traveling salesman, and probably ought to have been in show business. He could entertain. He was a dancer and was bubbling over with music. Never had a minute of musical training but he could play tunes on a mail-order harmonica.

It was never clear to me whether he even got out of high school but he could write a great story, if you didn't count off for spelling, and he was forever quick on the draw with a wisecrack.

He loved baseball for the opportunity it gave him to perform. He could sit in the stands behind home plate and keep half the crowd laughing with his remarks about the weakness of the umpire's vision. I can imagine now what the umpires thought of him.

He had a flock of eccentric habits. For years he traveled this state with a dog, a fox terrier named Danny McShane after the professional wrestler. When he stopped at a hotel he'd put that dog in a cardboard box, carry it in the lobby, set it up on the front desk, reach for a pen and start filling out a registration card while the dog watched from his box.

If the desk clerk announced that the hotel didn't take dogs, my father would nod, put the pen down and carry his dog out to look for another hotel. I was always amazed at the number of hotels that accepted the dog.

And this meant total acceptance. The dog not only slept in the room with my father, it also went to the coffee shop. And after dinner my father would throw a rubber ball in the lobby and bounce it off the walls and Danny McShane would make spectacular leaps and catch it. This was at a time when hotel guests sat reading and visiting in hotel lobbies in the evening and they were not always pleased with the dog show but this seemed not to bother my father at all.

For a person who made his living traveling, my father was a terrible driver. He was a clutch rider, and so his cars had bad clutches and always pulled away from stop signs bucking and pitching.

And yet, I admired and loved that man the most when we were in one of those old cars together. In summer when I was just a shirttail kid he would take me with him on one of his trips. We'd be rolling down a lonesome West Texas road. He'd turn the brim of his hat back and brace his bony knees against the wheel to steer, while he played "Springtime in the Rockies" or "Turkey in the Straw" on his harmonica.

This is what I think about on Father's Day. My old man.   ∽

Saying Goodbye to Max

My partner and I have come here to our country escape-place to say goodbye to one of the dogs, good old Max, who died a few weeks ago.

Since that sad event we've had his ashes in a sturdy container, waiting until we felt the time was right to spread his remains here and there over this little reservation where he spent his happiest days.

I'm giving you warning. This report will be a shameless outpouring of sentimentality about the loss of a dog. If you've never grieved about the death of a four-footed friend, probably you ought to turn the page and read something else.

We called him old Max but he wasn't old. He was seven. And he was poisoned, which is what makes his death so wrenching for us.

How he got hold of what killed him I don't know. If somebody did it on purpose, it's good that I don't know who it was because I would end up in a ton of trouble about it.

Old Max did himself a lot of hurting before he had to quit. He went out the hard way and we still feel his pain.

Because he never really understood about pain. Pain hurt his spirit, more than his body. When he was a pup we left him in a place to be trained. A month later we went to see what he had learned and a man brought him out on a leash and kept switching him to make him do what trained dogs do.

He responded by lying down and looking up and saying, "Why are you whipping me? All I want to do is be happy and love you."

We took him away from that place and he never got another switching. Or any training, either.

The beginning of Max, for us, happened at a benefit for the Houston Museum of Natural Science where they had this auction. One of the items was a yellow Lab pup, ten months old.

My partner fell in love with that pup from a distance of forty feet, and wanted it. I told her not to buy him because he was fox-faced, not a good Lab. We already had a dog, anyhow, a black Lab the size of a timber wolf.

She bought the pup anyhow.

In a dog show they wouldn't have let him in the door. What he would have won, though, was the grand championship of loving. He grew to ninety pounds of fierce muscle and became one of the best watch dogs I've known. He paid his keep.

But the way we'll remember him was how he showed his love. Several times a day he'd come up and stick his head in your stomach and push and then look up and tell you how much he loved you and how glad he was to live in your house.

He wasn't a ravenous eater. Give him his supper and he'd take a few bites and stop, and look up, and thank you for feeding him.

He loved this country place where he roamed among the trees on these ten acres and swam in the little creek. As long as you could throw his Frisbee he'd leap in the stock tank to retrieve it.

Probably I'll never stop seeing him paddling back to the bank, Frisbee in his mouth and a big grin in his eyes.

So we had this little private service for him here, and you may think it was sappy.

Half the ashes we spread over a section of the front yard where he spent so much time, lying with his head up and his front paws crossed. Watching over his place. Listening for significant sounds. Sniffing for good smells. Checking all vehicles that went by on the road, to be sure they didn't turn in the gate and invade his territory.

The ashes we had left we took down to the tank and broadcast them into that little body of water where old Max had such good times.

We did save a couple of handfuls that we flung under a post oak up close to the front gate. That was always the first stop Max made after he flew out of the pickup when we got here. Known to all in the family as Max's pee tree. We may put his marker there.

Both of us had a little speech made up to recite when we spread the ashes. But neither of us was able to say anything aloud without choking.

Me, I was just going to thank old Max for the time he spent with us, and tell him so long, and say how sorry I am that he had to endure all that pain. ❧

Burned Out

A couple of the customers have written to ask whatever happened to the chili peppers I used to raise.

You might say I got burned out on hot peppers.

I raised them for close to twenty years. Man, I had peppers up to my shoulder blades. I had flowerbeds bulging with 'em. I had peppers in pots on the window sills. Hanging from tree limbs. Sitting on top of the fence. All over the back yard. I had jalapeños and Tabascos and chiltipiquins and habaneros and cowhorns and cayennes and half a dozen other kinds that I don't even remember now.

Growing peppers was fun, but often demanding and confining. Every morning when I got up I'd go out with the first cup of coffee and check my plants, and wage war on bugs and spiders attacking my crop.

I bought books on chili peppers. I ordered seed and plants from far-away places, and they were delivered, and I planted them, and they grew, and made more peppers.

Once I even traveled to the city of Hatch, N.M., which is the chili pepper capital of this nation. In restaurants there I studied the ways in which people use peppers. I talked about peppers to gas station owners and cafe waitresses and people on the streets.

I bought a roomy wheeled cart to hold my plants that were especially sensitive to sunlight and/or shade, and I watched the sunlight and daily moved the cart so that the pepper plants received the proper amount of sun and/or shade.

My partner was tolerant, but she didn't really share my enthusiasm for peppers. I gave her recipes that demanded hot peppers. I brought her clippings from newspapers and magazines that told of the healthful benefits of hot peppers. How they throb with vitamins. How they are good for the heart.

I badgered her into using peppers in her kitchen. But I never converted her fully. She would chop up maybe half a jalapeño into a pot of soup, which is about like putting a pinch of salt into Lake Livingston.

When friends came to our house, I would make them go out and see my pepper plants.

"How did you get started raising peppers?" they'd ask, a polite question, the answer to which they weren't really interested in hearing. Well, that was just too bad. They shouldn't have asked it.

Because then they had to stand there and listen to me tell about being down in Mexico on assignment and making the acquaintance of the hotel clerk in the city of Veracruz. And how he took me home with him to meet his family, and I met his father-in-law, who was ninety-four and still healthy and strong. And his secret was that every day of his life he ate at least one raw, hot pepper. Chewed it up like half a handful of popcorn.

So that was the birth of my hot pepper career. I began raising them so I'd never be wanting for peppers, and since then, I've lived very few days without eating at least one.

"But what do you do with all these peppers?" people would ask. "You can't eat them all."

I loved to get that question. As quick as I heard it, I'd thrust upon its asker a double handful of fresh peppers, warning him about the funny-looking orange one there, which is a habanero and can burn blisters on a kitchen cutting board.

So that's what I did with my peppers—gave them away to anybody who'd take them.

For a long time, a good deal of construction went on in our neighborhood, and wherever you find construction in Houston you also find Hispanic workers who like hot peppers. I got rid of a ton of peppers that way.

When Maria the maid came to our house once a week, I always sent her home with a plastic bag of fresh peppers. At first she seemed delighted. After a few weeks she seemed less delighted. Then one afternoon when she was leaving the house, carrying her customary bag of jalapeños, I saw her quickly raise the lid on a garbage can, pitch the peppers in, and hurry on to catch her bus.

That was the beginning of the end, for me and my peppers. I still eat one every day, but I don't raise them any longer. ∾

Anybody Seen J.W.?

The other afternoon I needed to make a long distance call to a person in the little East Texas town of Leggett, which is on U.S. 59 a few miles north of Livingston.

I didn't have the number so I dialed directory assistance and talked to a woman who sounded like she was in New Jersey, or maybe Pennsylvania, and of course she had never heard of Leggett, and asked how the name is spelled.

Eventually she did find the number for me, so I am not criticizing the system, but that exchange got me thinking about the country telephone systems that were operating in this part of the world when I came to Houston in the late '40s.

My job then required me to do a lot of talking long distance to parties in small towns and on ranches and farms, and their phones were often on the lines of small local companies.

It was common for the office of such a company to be in a private home. Go in a house like that and you'd meet a friendly woman with a headset on, sitting before a switchboard bristling with wires and plugs. And this woman was personally acquainted with every phone customer the company had, and often knew where they were and what they were doing and why.

I made friends with as many of these operators as I could because they were valuable sources of local news and also because they were interesting women to know.

Say it's 1948 and I'm here in Houston and I want to talk on the phone to J.W. Somebody in a town about the size of Leggett or Glen Flora or Cat Spring. So I call his number and May, on the switchboard, tells me he's not at the house.

She says if it's important she might run him down before he leaves, that he's taking a load of calves to Houston this morning.

I tell her it's important and she says, "He's probably drinkin' coffee at the cafe about now. Hold on."

So I listen while she rings the cafe. A man answers with, "CA-fay." And May says, "Chester, is J.W. in there?"

"He just left, May," says Chester. "You might catch him at the lumber yard."

May says, "I thought he was haulin' calves to Houston today."

"Naw," Chester says, "he had transmission trouble on his truck. Said he was gonna buy staples and fix fence. How's your mama doin', May?"

"She had a pretty fair night, thanks. You know how it is. She has her good days and bad days. I'll check J.W. at the lumber yard."

I hear her ring the lumber yard. Man answers with, "Luhma yar." And May says, "Oscar, I'm lookin' for J.W."

Oscar says, "Haven't seen him this mornin', May. I think he's shippin' calves. Expect he's halfway to Houston by now."

"No, he didn't go. Had trouble with his truck."

"Aw. Well, that case, he might be at Riley's."

"He comes by there," May says, "tell 'im to call me, will you? How's Linda Sue? You a granddaddy yet?"

Oscar laughs, two gruff notes. "Not yet. She and Billy come by the

45

house last night. I swear I don't see how that girl's gonna last another fifteen minutes."

Riley's turns out to be the local auto repair shop.

"Mornin', Riley," May says. "J.W. happen to be in there?"

"Not yet, May, but I'm lookin' for him. Got his truck here. Listen, tell Jim his pickup is ready. Sittin' out front."

May says, "You gonna charge us another arm and a leg, I reckon."

"Naw, come on, wadn't nothin' much wrong with it. How come you married a man don't ever change his oil?"

"Whatta you talkin' about," May says, "I can't even get him to change his socks. When J.W. shows up, tell him to call me, OK?"

"OK. How's your mama doin', May?"

"Doin' pretty fair, thanks. Good days and bad, you know."

"Yeah, well, you tell her I said howdy. That's one of the best women I ever knew. Hey, hold on a minute, May. Guess who just rolled up. J.W. hisself."

So that's the way I'd find him, with the help of May at the switchboard and Chester at the CA-fay and Oscar at the luhma yar and Riley at Riley's.

Today it would be considered a slow and inefficient system but I loved it, and I miss it.   ∾

Babe Magnet

Digging in an old footlocker where I store a lot of leftovers from my previous lives, I turned up a snapshot of Red B., the greatest ladies man I ever knew.

This picture was taken in the desert south of Yuma, Ariz., in 1943. It shows Red leaning against the supporting pole of a basketball goal, on the Army Air Corps base where we were going to gunnery school.

When this shot was taken I'd known Red about a year, starting at Scott Field, Ill. He had the bunk next to mine and we got to know one another pretty well.

At Scott he had the reputation of forever being in some kind of minor difficulty. He would lose his cap just before inspection. Or he'd get a weekend pass to go into St. Louis and he wouldn't have any money. Or he'd be writing a letter in the day room and wouldn't have any notion of how to express the thought he wanted to convey.

And somebody would always help him. It was almost like we competed to help him, to see who could do the most for Red. I used to wonder why, and decided one reason was that he seem to need it so badly, and he was always appreciative and sincere about receiving the slightest help on any matter.

I was twenty-two then, and Red was a couple of years younger. To me he seemed fifteen, like a little brother.

Girls loved him. Seemed drawn to him. All of us liked to go into St. Louis with Red on Saturday night because he would attract girls and walk away with the prettiest one. Then the others of us could compete for what was left over.

We used to go to a place in St. Louis called Tune Town. It had two acres of dance floor and big bands played there, and unattached girls by the hundreds came to Tune Town to dance with the soldiers. That was a wonderful joint. I'll bet a few old grandfathers here in Houston remember going to Tune Town.

Say we'd been in that place a couple of hours and the band was resting and we'd all be sitting at a table, six of us, three girls and three guys. As far as the girls were concerned, there'd be only one guy at the table, and that was guess who. All three would be looking at Red with a sort of Mona Lisa smile, as if they waiting for him to look back at them or to say something to them.

I could have gotten up and announced that I was leaving because the club was on fire and the roof about to collapse, and those girls wouldn't have paid me the slightest notice because they were all busy looking at Red.

You may be saying, "Well, that Red must have been one handsome dude."

He was not. I would say he was what we then called baby-faced, with smooth slightly pink skin and big eyes, and he often kept on his face what I thought was an expression of bewilderment. As if he had just discovered that he was lost.

You read *Doonesbury*, I guess, the comic strip? Every once in a while Garry Trudeau draws a character with a look of bewilderment, with the eyebrows arched high. That expression makes me think of Red.

He wasn't any kind of cream puff, though. We played a lot of touch football at Scott, and Red had good hands. He could jump and catch a pass in a crowd and he had a sharp eye shooting a basketball, too.

St. Louis was a great soldier town during World War II. Through the USO we'd get invited to house parties, and I used to watch the reaction when we walked into a room. Red would go sit down on a sofa and look around with that sort of *I'm lost* expression and within five minutes he'd have girls beside him.

It was like he gave off some kind of invisible signal, or scent, that attracted females. Ask him how he did it and he'd pretend he didn't know what you were talking about.

From Scott we were shipped to gunnery school in the desert and I thought, well, in St. Louis with all its pretty girls Red was a great success but let's see how he does in Yuma, which had no more girls than it had rainfall, which was practically none at all.

But in Yuma he drew girls to him the same as in St. Louis, so I decided he was able to do it anywhere. That Red. I wonder whatever happened to him.   ∾

No Losers

A lot of people I know love to argue. Some had rather argue than eat. It's like they go around saying to friends, "Hey, how about let's get together tonight and have a disagreement?"

Sometimes, depending on the question they're debating, I can enjoy listening to the scrap but I'm not much on taking part. Mainly because I'm not so good at argument, and therefore can't enjoy it.

I know people who get such a boot out of a hot debate, they change physically. Their skin color deepens and their eyes glitter and they stand or sit straighter and most of them look just wonderful, when they're in the middle of an argument and they know they're doing a good job.

Early this month when a gang of us was on a fishing trip out in the Hill Country, camped on a river bank, a couple of our guys got into a flaming debate about gun control. In this state no other topic can raise passions higher and quicker. Not abortion. Not even football. I bet you could smell the smoke from that argument half a mile upstream.

We were hunkered down around a good fire after supper, feeling full and comfortable and glad to be on the river. Generally at such times we have stories, or maybe a few songs. But on this evening somebody happened to mention guns, and the word was a spark that set off a prairie fire.

It's interesting to watch a two-person argument develop, in a crowd. I'm always reminded of a scene that's common in nightclubs, or anyway it was back when I was going to nightclubs.

Maybe twenty couples move onto the floor to dance, and not long after the music begins, one couple in the middle of the floor starts doing intricate steps, and it's obvious they are fancy dancers. So gradually the other couples move away from the center of the floor to give the whirling pair more room to show off. And the two become performers, while all the other couples stand around to watch, and applaud when the music stops. This was once a frequent scene in bad movies.

The two-person debate we had on the river developed in that same way.

In the early going we had just a casual group discussion, with six or eight of us contributing comments. Then the two combatants began to emerge, talking a little louder than the group voice, and showing stronger opinions. And obviously on opposite sides of the question.

They were both thoroughly prepared, too, and were capable talkers, and so the others of us grew quiet, and sat back, and let the debaters perform.

Our evenings on the river don't usually run late because everybody is tired and ready to hit the blankets early, but that argument took up all the time we save for telling lies and singing songs and reciting bawdy limericks. It must have lasted two hours.

It was a good argument because the combatants are friends and they didn't get mad, or at least not much. But they did get loud.

When I saw the debate was sure to end in a draw, I sneaked away in the darkness and slid into my bedroll in the pickup and drifted off. Every few minutes I'd come awake when one of those guys lifted his voice to plead with his adversary to accept what any schoolchild knows is the proper position in the matter of gun control in this country.

I remember grinning into the night, thinking of the hoot owls and coyotes, pausing in their night's activities to wonder about the sound of those angry voices, echoing along the river.

Next morning I was a little relieved to find those two fellows sitting together by the fire, talking agreeably about the flavor of cowboy coffee, boiled in a granite-ware pot over a campfire.

I have to admit I was a little envious of them, having engaged in that vigorous argument. They may not have changed any minds but they did a good job presenting their cases and I suspect each of them felt like he'd come out the winner.

A little later that morning, down on the river, one of them told me that participating in the argument was the most fun he'd had in a month.　　　　　　　　　　　　　　　　　　　　　　　ॐ

A Song for Brother Roach

*M*y old friend Brother Robert C. Roach was buried Sunday in Bennett Cemetery near Apple Springs, not far from where he was born in the woods of Trinity County in 1907.

He lived ninety-two years, nine months and fifteen days.

Brother Roach spent his last years in a nursing home in Lufkin, playing his guitar and singing sweet songs for the ladies. He was a good musician and singer, but I'll remember him as the most prolific and best letter writer in my experience.

In all the years I've been in this business I've had several customers who wrote me on a regular basis but none wrote as often or as long or as well as Brother Roach.

I used to quote from his letters frequently and got in the habit of calling him Brother Roach in print. Journalism style wouldn't let me call him Mr. Roach on second reference, and I couldn't bring myself to refer to him as simply Roach.

So that's how the Brother title began, and he liked it.

Because of a promise I made twenty years ago I intended to drive to Lufkin for the funeral but some kind of weird bug got hold of me and laid me in the quilts. Instead of attending the service, I spent a few hours going through Brother Roach's letters, which I have saved.

I'm estimating the file contains around two hundred letters, written in a careful penciled script on yellow legal pad sheets. One of the last ones said he'd come down with Parkinson's disease and he apologized for the shaky handwriting.

"Early in my life," he wrote, "studying reading, writing and arithmetic, my teacher stressed the importance of writing a legible hand, otherwise it would be like speaking with a garbled tongue, and no one could understand it."

I thought I had all his letters but I haven't been able to locate two I especially remember. Probably I put them in a secret place, instead of in the regular Brother Roach file. Sometimes I hide things in a special place that way and then I forget where the place is.

Those special letters were about the little girl Brother Roach and his wife adopted, when they were past the age when people usually adopt. How they loved that child.

When she was old enough to ride they bought her a little bicycle and she hadn't had it two hours until she rode down the street and somebody took it away from her and ran off with it. The letter about that theft was the most elegant discourse on injustice I've ever read.

After that happened Brother Roach moved his wife and the girl out of the Houston area and went back to the Piney Woods, to Apple Springs where he originated. They hadn't been there long until that child was struck by an automobile on the highway and killed. The letter concerning that tragedy was a primal scream in the wilderness, about grief and the loss of a young life.

But most of the letters deal with his early times in rural East Texas, and about the things he'd seen and done during his long life. His experience was broad. He was a farmer, sawmill hand, master gardener, railroad clerk, bridge builder, truck driver, river boat deck hand, welder, horse breaker, storyteller and entertainer.

He often wrote about the food his family produced and consumed during his growing-up time in rural East Texas. Here's a letter about a dish called cush.

"I haven't eaten cush," he wrote, "since I was a young lad. Know what that stuff is made of? Leftover cornbread and cut-up green onions. Cush is all right if you like onions. It's a lot like dressing, without the blessing of turkey or chicken. (When he says dressing, he's referring to what most of us now call stuffing, as for a holiday bird.) One thing for sure, you better not go out on a date with a girl if you've been eating cush, unless she's been eating it as well. If you've both been eating it, neither of you will smell the onions. When I was dating girls, I'd put an onion in my pocket. If the girl had been eating cush I'd soon know it, and I'd nibble a little on my onion. You had to use strategy."

Brother Roach once wrote me a letter about an old hymn he called "Who Will Sing For Me?" The composer was a person who, like Brother Roach, often sang at funerals, and in the sad song he wondered,

> *When I cross that silent sea*
> *Who will sing a song for me?*

Brother Roach wondered in that letter who would sing a song for him when he died. I told him if nobody sang for him, if I was still here I'd sing one for him myself, and that seemed to please him.

After the funeral I talked to his niece, Elaine Lockhart at Apple Springs. She said hymns were played at the service but they were recordings.

So I owed Brother Roach a song, and I paid off. At the little country place in Washington County, I went down to the stock tank and sat on the dam and I sang the verses of "Precious Memories."

I didn't do any serious harm to that fine old hymn, because I was alone and nobody heard me. Except maybe my old friend Brother Robert C. Roach.   ॐ

He Didn't Take It Back

$\mathcal{W}$hile waiting in the dentist's office for my name to be called I found a magazine piece with a headline that told me in big black type, "You May Be Better Than You Think."

Message of the article was that both you and I are probably pretty good people, and very likely better than we suppose.

Then came an invitation to readers to recall in detail a situation in which we were faced with a decision to do what was right or wrong. Choose an event that happened early in your life, the article said, that you remember in detail. How you reacted at that time could indicate the direction you were headed in the matter of morals.

That interested me so I decided to give myself the test. I went all the way back to when I was in the third grade, and called up the time I rescued a valuable cap pistol that belonged to my friend Carter Wilkinson.

Carter was in my room at school. His father owned the dry goods store and therefore was very rich. Carter had bicycles. He had electric trains. He had all manner of other wonderful stuff. He collected things. Such as cap pistols.

He had dozens of cap pistols. He would bring some of them to school and make speeches about them and demonstrate the fast draw. He could twirl a cap pistol on his trigger finger the way Buck Jones and Tim McCoy did in the Saturday afternoon picture shows.

One day by mistake he left a cap pistol on the seat of his desk when he went home from school. It was a beautiful gun with a false pearl handle.

I told myself, "If this pistol stays here all night somebody might steal it." So I put it in my book satchel and took it home, as a favor to Carter Wilkinson.

In those times my father milked a Jersey cow in the back yard and we sold milk to neighbors. One of my chores was to go around and deliver this milk in fruit jars. Every night I went to the house where Carter Wilkinson lived because his mother was one of our milk customers.

On the way home from school with that neat pistol in my satchel, I told myself I would take the gun to Carter that evening when I delivered the milk.

At home I hid the gun in the feed room of the cow shed, a safe dry place. Stuck it back behind a bale of peanut hay and covered it with a couple of planks. I didn't want my father to see it because he would start asking questions.

He would know it wasn't my gun. A cap pistol like that, even then, would cost probably a dollar and a half, maybe more. At the time I'm talking about my family was not spending a dollar and a half on cap pistols, I promise you that. Not when we were selling Jersey milk, delivered by hand to the customer's ice box, for a dime per quart.

The first evening I wasn't able to return the pistol because my father was fixing the cow lot fence and would see me go in the feed room to get the gun. Told myself I would take it back the next day.

At Carter's house I put the milk in the ice box in the kitchen and then went in Carter's room. He was just putting away the pistols he had taken to school that day. He had a small trunk for those guns. It was half full of the things.

I asked him how many he had and he said he didn't know for sure. I asked if he ever lost one. He said probably he had but he didn't know because he had never kept a count on them.

The next evening I didn't take the pistol back as I'd planned. I don't remember exactly why. Maybe my father was out there again, still fixing fence.

I didn't take it back the next day, either, or the next. Because the truth is I wanted that gun for myself, really bad. After about two weeks I began thinking that it was mine, by rights.

Hadn't I saved it? Maybe so because if I hadn't taken it some other kid might have gotten it and he'd never have returned it to Carter. You understand I always intended to return the gun. At least I think I did.

The upshot of all this was that one day I went out to check the cap pistol and it was gone. Who got it, where it went, I don't know. For years afterward I debated with myself about that pistol. Had I really stolen it?

If so the crime didn't pay, because I never once got to use it in a game of cowboys and Indians.　　　　　　　　　　　　　　　　　　ᢙ

Fist City

About four o'clock in the afternoon I was driving east through Memorial Park and saw a fistfight going on.

I am not in favor of fistfights, but if one is already in progress I don't mind slowing down a minute to watch. Most such fights are brief, and have no lasting significance.

The participants in this one looked to be maybe fifteen. Both male, if I need to say so. Many boys of that age are full of vinegar and don't need much of an excuse to start trouble.

You would think, since they are so eager to do battle, that they'd learn a little something about how to fight, but few ever do. I am judging by the school-ground and city-park fistfights I've seen over the years, when the fighters are mad at one another. I've seldom seen a jab thrown, or any sign of a defensive tactic.

What they do is flail away with roundhouse swings that don't usually land, or else they strike shoulders and arms and the sides of skulls. Then comes the lunge, when one fighter tackles the other and they both go rolling and grunting and kicking. A combination of boxing and wrestling. Really ugly to watch.

This sort of action is physically taxing, and as a rule both fighters are ready to quit pretty soon. Which is what happened there in Memorial Park. Several observers were on hand, and some of those stepped in as peacemakers.

This was the first fight I'd seen in several years. The previous one was in New Orleans.

My partner and I were walking with the crowd along Bourbon Street, and these two young guys suddenly began hitting each other, right there in the middle of the parade.

Street fights of this kind require a lot of room, much more than the participants would have if they were in a boxing ring. As a spectator you need to be nimble and ready to move, or else you might get mixed up in the action.

That Bourbon Street fight was among the shortest I've seen. It didn't go half a round, and I couldn't tell that one punch hit anything but air.

It does interest me, that chesty young guys like this walk around looking for a fight and then when they find one, they don't need more than a minute of it before they've had enough.

I've become convinced that the main danger of injury in fighting of this kind has to do with where the battle takes place. The grass of Memorial Park is probably a good place, if there's a choice.

The worst place, I think, is indoors.

I watched a fight one time in a dance hall, back when I was doing a lot of my work after dark. About 11:30—often a sensitive hour for tempers in dance halls on Saturday nights—a couple of guys began flailing away, knocking each other down.

This was not a pretty fight, and I became concerned that both of the combatants would be seriously injured. Not from being hit by fists but from falling over the furniture.

Like folding chairs. A guy gets shoved down and catches the seat of a folding chair across the small of his back, that's got to hurt. This is not breakaway furniture like they have in barroom brawls in the movies. When the fight's over and friends help the loser walk away, he's probably not hurting from a fist blow but from something he fell on.

The strangest fistfight I ever saw was back in the '60s when I used to tag along every year on the Salt Grass Trail.

Beside the road there was this pickup, with two guys in the cab. The window on the right-hand side was down. A third guy stood beside the open window, crying and punching the bejabbers out of the passenger in the cab.

The guy getting punched did not fight back. He sat there and kept getting punched. Driver of the pickup evidently didn't want to get involved. He didn't move the truck. Just let his passenger sit and be punched. After a while, the puncher stopped punching and walked away, wiping his tears.

As strange a scene as that was, I can understand the puncher's crying. Anger is a highly emotional state, and sometimes generates tears.

From playground games long ago I remember boys we used to avoid when they cried, because they were the meanest when they started shedding tears.

How He Ended Up

The other afternoon I was in what we used to call a butcher shop, and one of the butchers in there was a dead ringer for my Uncle Barney, who has been gone now for I guess twenty-five years.

I'm not talking about vague family resemblance. Or favor, as people used to say: "Edgar sure favors his daddy." Meaning Edgar looks a lot like his father.

This fellow in the butcher shop didn't just favor our Uncle Barney, my father's younger brother. To me, he was Uncle B's reincarnation. Slender. About five-ten. A sort of athletic slouch about his posture. The same sleepy eyes. And the droopy grin that produced a look of dissipation. Something like the actor Peter O'Toole.

I loved Uncle Barney as much as I did my own father. But the idea that he might be reincarnated as a butcher doesn't fit. Because Uncle Barney was a gambler.

In my growing-up time, I was proud of him. He gave me standing among my peers. Other kids would brag that their fathers were railroad engineers or firemen or policemen or cowboys. I could shut them up by saying that my uncle was a gambler.

Not just occasionally. Gambling is what he did for a living. And like most gamblers I've known, he was sometimes flush but more often broke.

He never had a home that I knew anything about. He roamed, in constant search of what he called "a pretty nice little game."

During the Great Depression he'd show up at our house every few months. Sometimes he'd be driving a nice car. The next time he'd have a junker that smoked like a wood stove. The next time he'd be walking. The next time he'd have a nice car again, and new shoes.

He'd stay a few days, and one morning he'd get up early and leave without saying goodbye.

Before I got old enough to know better, I admired Uncle Barney's lifestyle. It seemed romantic, adventurous. Wandering over the country. Meeting all sorts of interesting folks. Never putting down roots. Playing cards for a living. And he seemed happy to me. Always grinning. Making jokes.

One summer just after World War II began, my family moved to San Angelo where a bombardier training base was being built. Almost anybody could walk in the front gate of that base and get a job that paid four or five bucks a day. Thousands of men flocked there, eager for work.

I worked at that base as a lumber checker the summer before I went in the Army. My father worked there. A couple of my uncles, as well. One day who should walk up but Uncle Barney. Did he intend to take a job out at the base? Not quite. When the men left the next morning for work, Uncle Barney went the other way, toward town.

Late that afternoon I was sitting on the front steps, waiting on supper, and here came Uncle Barney slouching up in the yard. He stopped, grinning at me, and pulled out of his pants pocket a wad of cash so large he had trouble holding it in one hand.

"Found a pretty nice little game in town," he said.

He stayed around a few days—I suppose until the nice little game got not so nice—bought a used car and disappeared. I wanted to go with him.

Because even then, when I was twenty-one, I still admired his life. I was working all day for four bucks and there was Uncle Barney sitting in a pool hall playing cards and making in one afternoon more money than I had ever seen before.

But gradually, over the years as I learned more about his life than he showed on the surface, I lost that admiration. I believe now his grin was hiding a tragic life. Broken family. No real home, ever. Countless lonely, desperate nights.

One of the last times I saw him he was getting old. He came to Houston on a bus, and asked me to drive him to a warehouse off North Main. Said he was trying to acquire a crap table that was rigged so that the roll of the dice could be controlled remotely. I was relieved when he came out of the warehouse empty-handed.

I still loved him because I couldn't help it, but I was saddened to see how he ended up—still searching for the pretty nice little game.   ∽

Skin Game

*T*oday I'm thinking about the swimming pool in the city park, back in my old hometown.

The reason is, last week I stayed out in the sun too long without adequate cover and got blistered. I'm now peeling off like a boiled potato, and wearing long sleeves all day so the public won't think I have some kind of infectious disease.

This takes me back to the swimming pool because in my early times that body of water was Sunburn City. As soon as school was out, practically everybody in town between the ages of eight and eighteen headed for the swimming pool to get the color of their skin changed.

I am talking here about the 1930s, when word reached our town that turning brown in the summer was in fashion. We all wanted that popular skin color.

We had this new swimming pool as a place to gather and burn ourselves, and the price of admission was only twenty cents. The pool was a great curiosity and drew large crowds.

Most of us had never before seen a swimming pool with a concrete bottom. We were accustomed to swimming in creeks and stock tanks and so it was a great luxury to paddle around in a pool that didn't have water moccasins or crawdads in it.

I don't believe dermatology had been invented then, or if it had the word had not come to our town. No doctors told us that roasting our hides was dangerous, and could cause skin cancer. In fact, when you got yourself tanned about the color of a new saddle you were thought to be healthy, and everybody would tell you how fine you looked. Even the doctor would tell you that.

In order to become properly burned, we endured a four-phase treatment.

In Phase I, everybody put on a bathing suit and lay out under the blazing sun for several hours. When we couldn't stand the heat any longer we'd jump in the water and cool down. Then get back out and lay on the bank for more burning.

I'll bet when Phase I was in its peak hour, a person with a sensitive nose could have walked around that pool and smelled flesh cooking.

Phase II began at bedtime, the first night following Phase I. Everybody was sick, their skin ranging in color from a warm pink to a flaming red. Some would run a fever. They couldn't stand for as much as a sheet to touch their skin.

This second phase might last several days. The victims would be up and around but you'd see them holding their bodies in an exceptional way, exactly vertical, so their clothes would hang loose and wouldn't rub any skin.

And they tended to shy away from friends who might pat them on the shoulder as a greeting. Because a pat almost anywhere on that fried skin was torture.

Phase III was peeling time. The injured top layer of their hide had died and all the tanning candidates sat around peeling dead skin. This could get gross and yet there was something fascinating about pulling sheets of hide off yourself and it didn't hurt.

One summer my Cousin Eugene Autry became a local celebrity by performing a Phase III miracle. He had thin fair skin and in Phase I he had taken a really dreadful burn. He suffered mightily. I thought he would never cure enough to peel.

Then one afternoon he was on the front porch and he suddenly began losing that burned hide and within a few minutes he got rid of his entire outer covering. He shed all his skin like a snake does and walked away from it, looking pink and new, and left his old skin in a pile there on the porch. Up to that time I had never seen anything as wonderful.

Phase IV was critical. This was when the peeled victims decided how long to wait before they exposed their new tender skin to the sun, hoping for tan instead of red. Some were able to succeed, and became smooth and beige and the doctor chaperoning the Friday night dance would say they looked outdoorsy and healthy.

But others would go out too soon and get sunburns on top of their sunburns, and fry again, and peel again. And sometimes in August you would see people around the swimming pool that looked like lepers. Their shoulders would show parts of three and four layers of burned skin, all raw and terrible, and you wondered why they didn't put on their clothes and go home and stay out of the sun.　　　◌

A Matter of Perspective

A rainy day. Cold. A day good for staying inside by the fire.

But I was out and around. Driving toward downtown, I was stopped by a traffic light. Standing in the rain at the intersection was one of our city's street beggars. Their tribe is increasing.

This one was looking cold and unhappy. Man of about forty, I'd guess. Not a small person but he had this slump-shouldered way of standing, so that he seemed harmless and somehow wounded.

Across his chest he held the usual light brown cardboard sign, looked like it had been torn from a box he fished out of a Dumpster. Two bold words on the sign: HOMELESS. HUNGRY.

I had a passenger. Call him Friend. He's always telling me not to put his name in the paper, so I won't. A lot of my friends are that way.

Before the light changed, Friend dug a $5 bill out of his wallet and passed it over and told me to give it to the guy standing in the rain.

Which I did, and the little person seemed highly pleased, and thanked us kindly, and asked God to bless us.

We pulled away and I wondered why. Why did Friend give money to a fellow like that?

"Because he's homeless," Friend replied, "and hungry, like his sign said."

I said yeah, but what if he's just a bum who doesn't want to work, and he's not really homeless and hungry?

"He looked homeless and hungry to me," Friend said.

But didn't Friend understand that this is how these panhandlers make a living? Didn't he know that these guys stand out there looking pitiful so we'll feel guilty and give them money? It's a scam, man.

"Are you sure?" Friend asked. "That may be true in some cases. Maybe even most. But how about the guy who's really down and out, and doesn't have a dime to buy a doughnut, and he's out there on the street asking for his next meal?"

I said we have places in our city where people like that can be fed, and given a place to sleep. You pay taxes. You give to United Way.

"But you still have people who work the streets," Friend said.

Why?

"I don't know why. Maybe they take what they can get from welfare and it's not enough and they get out on the street and beg."

But why don't they go to work? That fellow Friend gave five bucks to back there? I bet that within six blocks of that intersection, you'd find a dozen help-wanted signs in windows.

Friend was shaking his head, grinning. He said, "Have you ever been out of a job?"

Well, no, not really.

"You never have walked into a place that needed help and asked for a job?"

No, never have done that.

"If you did," Friend said, "probably you'd need to pass a physical. Have you ever had a communicable disease?"

Well, sure, like a bad cold.

"No, I mean like syphilis, gonorrhea, stuff like that."

No.

"Do you have a police record?"

Not far as I know.

"You've never been arrested?"

Not exactly. Told him I'd been pulled over by the cops a few times, for going too fast, or because my taillights were burned out.

"But you've never been taken to town, to the police station, and booked?"

No.

"Never spent a night in jail?"

No, not unless he wanted to count the night I spent in the old Austin County Jail in Bellville that time, as a charity stunt to help raise money for a museum.

"I won't count that," Friend said. "But any of that other stuff, if it's on your record it's not easy just to walk up and get work."

Did he mean to say that all these folks holding cardboard signs at traffic lights are unemployable?

"No," Friend said, "but I'm saying some of them are. And I'm saying that fellow back there deserved a little help. I judged by the look on his face."

So he invested $5, on the chance that he was right.

"Tell you something else," Friend said, after we were downtown and parked, "whether you deserve help or not, standing out in the rain, hoping somebody will give you a buck, is not easy work."

He sounded to me like somebody who'd had experience in that line. But I decided not to ask.   ❧

Pesky Punctuation

Some of the mail lately has been about the apostrophe problem.

I'm convinced that nine out of ten citizens aren't bothered by the trouble apostrophes cause in this world, maybe because they're not even aware of it.

But that one person among the ten is particular about rules of punctuation, and when he or she sees the apostrophe misused, he or she cries out in anguish, and pulls his or her hair, and smites the Earth in frustration. This is the sort of person who writes to newspaper columnists about the apostrophe problem.

I can offer you a quick test to take, if you want to find out whether or not you are part of this problem that pollutes the written American language:

Say you're driving along and you see a sign saying, "Goat's For Sale." A mile later you see another saying, "The Stewart's Live Here." Farther along you see a third that says, "Watermelon's."

71

If you don't see anything the matter with those signs, you are part of the apostrophe problem. Because all three signs are wrong. None of them should have an apostrophe.

The only way I can think of that "Goat's For Sale" could be counted correct is, if the "Goat's" is read as a contraction of "goat is." Then the sign would be saying, "Goat Is For Sale." Which seems to say that only one goat is offered and I doubt that's what the goat seller meant. Most people who sell goats want to sell more than one.

In this nation's misty past, somebody must have spread the rule that when the plural form of a noun ends with the letter *s*, an apostrophe goes before the *s*.

The idea caught on, big time, and so we have people still writing "goat's" when they mean to refer to more than one goat, and "watermelon's" when they mean an entire truck load of watermelons.

In 1952, along with the woman I was married to then, I built a house in Bellaire, on Valerie Street. One day when nobody was watching, a guy came along that street and spray-painted on the curb the names of the families who lived in every house. Then he returned later and asked each homeowner for $2.

I refused to pay because he had sprayed on our curb the words "The Hale's." He also had put "The Hausinger's" and "The Miller's" and "The Baker's" on the curb of our neighbors.

When he returned I explained to him that he had spread unnecessary apostrophes throughout our neighborhood. He did not understand what I meant. I tried to explain to him why the apostrophes were wrong but I couldn't get my message across.

I asked him why he put the apostrophes in those names and he said that was the way he was taught, when he was in school many years before.

So I didn't argue, because he may have been right.

Back in the '60s I took money several years for teaching a couple of writing courses to college students. A high percentage of them would write "goat's" when they meant more than one goat. I marked that kind of error a thousand times but the day before I stopped teaching I was still getting stories containing that same apostrophe problem.

For twenty-something years I campaigned in the column to get the apostrophe problem corrected. I used to take pictures of signs that said things like "Watermelon's For Sale" and "Angora Goat's" and put them in the paper. I also printed examples of all the other ways I found the apostrophe being used wrong, in newspapers and magazines. Sometimes even on neon signs.

But it seemed to me that the more I advertised the apostrophe problem the worse it got, and finally I gave up and quit.

My position now on the matter is that the apostrophe—except for certain specialized uses—should be outlawed altogether, on the ground that the rules governing its use are not enforceable.

But I still have a stern personal policy relative to the problem. I refuse to do any business at a roadside stand if its sign says "Watermelon's." And if I ever see a sign that says "Goats" instead of "Goat's," I may stop and buy a couple. ❧

Country Editor

When I went back to the old home town for a reunion recently, one of my former classmates told me I never should have left that place.

"You ought to have stayed here," she said, "instead of going off and writing for a big city newspaper. You could have bought the local weekly and been a country editor. You'd have had a lot more fun."

That might be true, but I'm not sure. All the country newspaper editors I've known, if they made a decent living, worked their tails off. Sometimes seven days a week.

I once had a chance to become a country editor. I'd been out of school less than a year and I'd taken a sort of press agent job I didn't like. Then I heard about a country newspaper opportunity in a dusty little town up in the Panhandle, and I thought that might be what I wanted to do with my life.

The gent who had that weekly was getting old, or thought he was. He was looking for a young fellow to come in and work with him, for almost no pay, and eventually buy the paper.

This was 1946 and the best newspaper job I'd been offered came from the *Lubbock Avalanche-Journal.* The editor told me he'd try to make a reporter out of me—for $30 a week. I walked away. I could have done a lot better than that by staying in the Army.

The idea of running a country weekly appealed to me. I had the notion that if a guy worked hard and did the job in a unique way, the world might come to his door. He could be famous. He might even make money.

A few Texas country editors proved that this idea had possibilities. Henry Fox, starting as the editor of the *Madisonville Meteor,* became a nationally syndicated columnist. Over in the Big Thicket, Arch Fullinjim at the *Kountze News* became nationally known as an eccentric country editor who composed his stories on a Linotype machine.

However, I needed about thirty minutes to see that I'd have never survived at that weekly up in the Panhandle. I didn't know enough. I had a degree in journalism but that wouldn't get me to first base at being an editor and publisher.

The fellow who ran that paper was worn out, and he wasn't anywhere near old as I am now. He ran the place almost without help. He wrote the stories. Set them on Linotype. Set the headline type by hand. Made up the pages and locked them in the metal forms and put them on a flatbed press and operated the press and, with the help of a grandson, even delivered the paper.

Then, when he ran out of something to do, he went hiking around town, hustling ads.

Well. I could have learned to do all that but I didn't want to, and thought I didn't have time. I wanted to be a country editor who wrote funny and folksy stuff that would draw the attention of New York syndicates. I sure didn't want to sell ads or run a press.

Another thing, that Panhandle editor had one regular employee, a woman about sixty who answered the phone, read proof, and wrote a

Page One column called "Goings On About Town," or something similar. She produced items like, "Mr. and Mrs. Horace McSwill Sr. visited their son and daughter-in-law, Mr. and Mrs. Horace McSwill Jr., in Amarillo on Sunday."

Furthermore, that woman didn't like me, I could tell. I was twenty-five then but I already knew that her being sixty didn't mean she was approaching retirement. She'd be sitting there writing that column when she was eighty, and sticking commas in my copy and changing my adjectives when she read proof. And even if I owned the paper I'd be afraid to fire her.

But sometimes I think about how my life would have been if I'd found the right place to be a country editor. Some of those old boys became big frogs in their small ponds, and they loved it.

I think about my friend the late Franz Zieske, editor of the *Bellville Times*. When a fire in or around Bellville was reported, the volunteers drove the fire truck to the *Times* office. There they slowed down enough for Zeiske to come out and swing aboard, so he could ride to the scene and cover the fire.

I always suspected that sort of thing was what Zeiske loved most about being the editor of a country newspaper.   ∾

Listening Skills

They keep telling me that what makes a marriage work is communication, so my partner and I try to communicate the best we can.

The trick is in developing common interests, so that both partners can engage in meaningful conversations. The other morning I recorded the following dialogue that took place in our house just after breakfast.

I was the first speaker in this exchange. While reading the paper I said, "Well, I see that Clements got his fifth win already."

My partner was staring at the furniture. Her response to my remark was, "This room seems stark. I wonder how a couple of red pillows would look on the white sofa."

I replied, "At the rate he's going, the Rocket could easily win twenty games this season, at age forty-two. How about that?"

She said, "All these books need to be taken out of the shelves and dusted and rearranged."

So I said, "Do you realize that the Astros could have three twenty-game winners this year? If it happens that ought to put us in the World Series, unless those hot bats cool down in the playoffs again."

And she said, "I'm going to get those Muscles For Hire men out here again to wash all these windows."

"That Biggio," I said, chuckling, "he's a piece of work. Plays like he hasn't lost a step, and still looks like a college boy."

By then she was standing at a window, staring into the back yard, and her response was, "The Lady Banks at the corner of the house needs pruning or it's gonna be the plant that ate Houston. Oh, look at my Cecile Bruner. She has lots of new little roses this morning. But I need to go out there with my squirt bottle and get after those thrips."

Then I said, "Check this box score. Talk about offense. Against the Reds last night we had seven .300 hitters in the lineup. Even early in the season like this, that's pretty remarkable."

She said, "What's today, Wednesday? Do you know I have to give a review tomorrow and I'm not half through that book?"

My answer to that was, "The way I see it, so far I'd say the most improved player on our roster is Adam Everett. He covers the real estate out there, man, and moves so pretty. Swingin' the bat, too. Wouldn't you agree he's improved more than anybody else on the team?"

She replied, "We haven't had fish for a week. Think I'll do a snapper for tonight."

"Look at this," I said. "Bagwell went three for five against Cincinnati and he's hitting .333 now. And he's always saying he's not quite comfortable at the plate. If he ever gets comfortable up there he ought to out-hit Ted Williams."

And she said, "Wait a minute. I've got a dental appointment so I might not feel like cooking. We could go out. Would you mind?"

My response was, "The only reason we got swept by the Cardinals the other night was that bad call at third base. Otherwise we'd have won that game. All the TV replays showed the runner was safe. You know, I might be in favor of replay officiating, like in football. Bad call like that could cost us the pennant, man."

I thought that was a fairly interesting proposal. When I made it she was looking at a magazine and she replied, "I'm thinking about signing up for art classes. Pastels, maybe. I'm interested mainly in color. What do you think?"

I told her, "If I was young and just now starting out in the newspaper business, I'd be a sports writer."

You see what I mean about communicating? You just have to work at it a little bit. ❧

The Wild West

$\mathcal{I}$n the 1880s my Uncle Billy Crockett was a cowboy on trail drives from West Texas up to Kansas.

In the 1930s he was maybe the same age as I am now, and had been settled for forty years up in Palo Pinto County. When I knew him, what he did mostly was sit on the front porch and wait for supper. But in the family he had a reputation of being a salty cowboy in his youth.

By that time my cousins and I had been to town to see a few Buck Jones and Tim McCoy movies, and we would try to get Uncle Billy to tell hairy stories about trail driving in the old days. He almost always disappointed us because his experiences on the trail weren't anything like what we saw in the cowboy movies.

We wanted to hear him talk about stampedes, when a thousand head of Longhorns would jump up in the middle of the night and go charging across the prairie and the cowboys would ride like the wind to turn the leaders and keep the whole herd from flying off the rim of a canyon 500 feet deep.

"I never seen nothin' like that," Uncle Billy would say, and then ask: "Why would a bunch of steers jump up in the middle of the night and go runnin' off somewhere?"

We'd say it was always because of a thunderstorm. Lightning would strike a dead tree close to where the herd was bedded, and the cattle would get up and stampede. At least that's the way it happened in the horse operas we'd seen on Saturday afternoon in town.

Uncle Billy would say, "Well, I rode up to Kansas twice, and I never saw no stampedes. You take three or four hundred steers and they've been walkin' fifteen or twenty miles ever day for a month, by sundown they're all so blamed tired you can't get 'em into a trot, much less a run."

Understand I am trying here to reconstruct Uncle Billy's speech the best I can. His exact words are no longer in my head, but I do remember how he talked and what he said, in a general way.

We'd ask, "But what would happen when the terrible storms came on the trail, in the middle of a dark night?"

"Truth to tell, boys," Uncle Billy would say, "I don't recollect no storms. On my first trip we took 500 steers from Shackelford County to Kansas and it never rained a drop the whole way. I'd have give half my pay to hear a thunderclap and feel a shower of rain."

"How about when Indians attacked?" we'd ask.

"Well, we'd see a few Indians sometimes, squaws mostly, and children, up in Oklahoma, but they was all afoot and lookin' pitiful. Some would camp, out a ways from the herd, and the cook would give 'em beans and biscuit."

"And they never did attack?"

"Naw."

We'd want to hear him talk about going into Dodge, and seeing all those gun battles in the street, and the fist fights in the saloons, and the drunk cowboys shooting up the mirrors behind the bar and going upstairs with the dance hall girls. All that good stuff we'd seen at the picture show about the cowpokes celebrating at the end of the trail.

"Well, I never got what you'd call into downtown Dodge," Uncle Billy would say. "We got close to the railroad, we'd bed down and wait for a cow buyer to come out, and not a one of us in camp had half a dollar to go into town with. We never got paid till the steers got sold, and by then we'd be past ready to come home and we'd just head on back. Fact is by the time we got to Kansas, I was so wore out I didn't feel like doin' no celebratin' "

He never saw a gunfight?

"Naw. The bunch I was with, they never had no guns to fight with. Where they gonna get twenty spare dollars to buy a gun?"

Did Uncle Billy himself carry a gun on the trail?

"Naw."

In all those miles of trail driving, did he ever get shot at?

"Naw." Then he lifted a hand. "Well, I did, too, once. We was comin' home, and crossed the Red into Wilbarger County. I was pushin' an old lead steer they wanted back at the place, and some way he got away from me and trotted up in the yard of a farm house and hooked two bedsheets off a clothesline, and a woman come out of that house and let fly at me with both barrels of a shotgun."

Did she hit him?

"Naw," Uncle Billy said.   ∾

A Long Way Down

$\mathcal{T}$he last time I went back to my old hometown I drove out to the city lake to visit the bridge where I learned a lesson that has served me well for more than sixty years.

I was disappointed to discover the bridge is gone, replaced by a better one not half as interesting. The old one was a wood-floored metal truss bridge that spanned a narrow channel in the lake. It was a popular place to fish because we thought that sooner or later all the fish in the lake would pass under that bridge.

Which probably wasn't true but we used to catch pretty good channel cat and crappie out of that channel and in summer a little gang of fishermen was almost always gathered there.

Most of us were fifteen or sixteen, when we were beginning to broaden out a little in the shoulders and to cuss and spit through our front teeth and walk sort of apelike, with our arms held away from our sides.

One hot summer afternoon we were fishing at the bridge and weren't getting any action and I made a smart-aleck remark. I said what I'd like to do was crawl up on the top of one of those trusses and dive off, and get cool.

One of the guys said, "Well, go ahead, do it."

I said I would if I was sure the deputy sheriff wouldn't come by and catch me swimming. That lake was the town's water supply and it was against the law to swim in it, or so we thought. If such a law did exist it was often violated in certain locations where willow trees provided a little cover.

"You wouldn't dive off that truss," my companions said. "You haven't got the guts."

I considered myself a pretty fair swimmer and diver then. In fact, one of my ambitions was to become an Olympic diver and I had spent a good deal of time practicing swans and jackknives at the municipal pool.

One of the gang said, "Go on, if you're such a hot diver. I dare you."

Well, a dare was a serious matter. You had to take the dare or back down, and backing down was bad for the reputation. If you backed down from a dare, the word got around.

I want to say the top of one of those trusses was about eight feet from the floor of the bridge. Then in summer the lake was low, so from the bridge floor down to the water was probably another eight feet.

Sixteen feet didn't seem like much height, so I took the dare.

But on one condition. I said if those guys would come back out there at dawn the next morning, when there wasn't much chance of a law officer seeing me do it, I'd dive off the bridge just before sunrise.

I slept pretty well that night because I didn't think they would get up that early and walk out to the lake. It was a couple of miles outside the city limits.

However, three of them showed up.

It was a moist morning, with patches of fog on the water. I shucked off, down to my shorts, and climbed the truss and stood up. I think the month was August but that early in the morning, standing up there in my underwear, I was cold.

The water looked black, and little napkins of fog scooted over the surface. Those sixteen feet looked like 800.

"Well," they said, "whatcha waitin' for? Go ahead."

I said I heard a car coming and I got down off the truss and grabbed my pants and waited for the car.

"Ain't no car comin'," they said.

No car came so I took my pants off and climbed the truss again. I sure hated to go back up there.

I almost did it. Once I was leaning, close to the point of no return, but I saw something moving down on the water, a kind of wiggle. A snake, maybe. I sure didn't want to dive onto a cottonmouth moccasin so I stalled.

Maybe, when I couldn't stall any longer, maybe I'd have done it. I've never been certain. But when I seemed close to going off the truss one of the guys said these beautiful words:

"Hey, don't do it. You're liable to dive off there and hit a stump and break your neck. Come on down."

I looked at the others and they nodded agreement and that released me from the stupidity of taking the dare.

That experience taught me something ever so valuable, and this is the rule I carried away from the old bridge:

Before you say you'll do something foolish that only your ego demands that you do, think about how high it is from the top of the bridge down to the water. ∽

But He Wants Birds

*Y*ou've caught me playing with my birthday presents.

Right now I'm seasoning my new cast-iron Dutch kettle. It's a vessel of great beauty, with three stubby little legs. The lid is heavy and flat and has a raised edge all around the rim for holding hot coals on top.

I'm really pleased with this present. It's for campfire cooking. I can fix stew in it, or beans, or make cornbread. Maybe even a decent peach cobbler if I practice a few times.

To season a new cast-iron vessel you bathe it in olive or cooking oil and put it in your oven for about an hour at 350. Then cut the heat off and leave the pot in there until the oven cools.

This is a serious pot, weighing seventeen pounds on my bathroom scales.

Another birthday present I got is a bird feeder of a sort I'd never seen before. It's supposed to be squirrel-proof. And it's adjustable, so you can keep certain undesirable birds from eating out of it. Pretty neat.

I've got it hanging from a limb of the Mexican plum in the back yard. It looks like a small house. On each of its sides is a perch bar where the birds can light to feed. The perch is hinged at both ends. This is the part that's adjustable.

I have it adjusted to shut out blue jays, grackles, starlings and birds of similar size that I'm not much interested in subsidizing. Say a blue jay lands on one of the perches. He's too heavy so the perch swings down, and this causes a sturdy metal band to descend and cover the grain. Long as that perch is depressed, bird can't get to the seed.

Cardinals aren't heavy enough to depress the perch so they can sit there and eat. So can some of the other small birds that I like to have around. So can the house sparrows but there's nothing to be done about those. They're just here, to stay.

I wouldn't mind feeding blue jays if they weren't so brassy and de-structive. They seem mainly interested in scaring off other birds and scattering what grain they don't eat. I was interested in seeing how long it would take the jay birds to figure out this fancy feeder.

It took two days. Finally they learned that if they tried to light on the perch the metal band would shut off access to the feed. So what they do is hover, wings beating furiously, and without touching the perch they poke their beaks in and gobble a few sunflower seeds on the fly.

But they don't eat a lot that way because it's too much work. They do manage to knock a lot of grain out of the feeder but that's OK because the doves are there on the ground waiting for it to fall and they clean it up.

It took the squirrels a little longer.

My attitude toward squirrels has mellowed in recent times. I have fought those condemned bushy-tailed rodents until finally I'm simply tired fighting. But I got a kick out of seeing them puzzle over this feeder.

They'd come off the limb and get on the feeder's roof and then drop onto the perch, which would immediately shut off access to the goodies. They'd sit there and you could see the question marks on those rat-like faces. Now what kind of a rig is this?

Then they'd gnaw, and claw, but the feeder is made of stout metal and

87

it's slick, without many places to cling to, and a lot of the squirrels would slip and go twisting down in the azalea bushes.

Squirrel lovers don't need to worry. The fall didn't hurt any of them. I've seen squirrels fall out of a forty-foot pecan tree and hit the ground in a high lope.

Here's how they finally won: Squirrel gets on top of the feeder. Takes a firm grip on the edge of the roof with his rear claws. Lets his body then swing down the side of the feeder without touching the perch. Then he hangs there, inverted, and eats till he's full.

Maybe they'll get tired of eating upside down, but I doubt it.　ॐ

It's Not KFC

*H*ere's a letter signed only as Suzy O. She writes to ask if I have ever chopped off the head of a chicken.

She says her five-year-old daughter was recently told, by her grandfather, that long ago people would catch a chicken and chop off its head and pluck out its feathers and cut it up and cook it for dinner.

The child refused to believe that nice people would ever do that to a harmless chicken.

Nice people did do that, of course, and I could take you to places where they still do.

But I can see that five-year-olds would have a hard time believing such a thing, before they're exposed to all the bloody violence they'll be watching on television. I expect that when they're eleven or twelve, they'll be bored by the sight of a chicken getting its head chopped off, since probably by then they've already seen human heads severed in living color.

I will leave it to the psychiatrists to tell us when it's all right to tell little children that the drumsticks they eat came off chickens killed in the prime of their lives. Or that the meat in their hamburgers was once part of a dead cow that had pretty eyes like Elsie.

Most of us with gray heads and rural backgrounds never had any trouble accepting that we were eating the meat of dead animals because we were exposed early on to the killing. It was a part of our daily life.

One of my earliest memories was watching my father wring the neck of a chicken. This was not on a farm, not at that time. It was in the middle of town—not a very big one—where my father worked in a dry goods store.

He'd come home for lunch and before he went back to the store he'd often go out in the back yard and catch a frying chicken. He'd be wearing nice clean clothes and his shoes would be shined but he was expert in the matter of catching excited chickens. We always raised fryers in the back yard if we were living in a place with a chicken-proof fence.

He'd grab a bird by the neck and twist fiercely, and it always reminded me of the way he cranked our old Chevy, except he twisted faster and the circle of his twist was tighter, and pretty soon off came the head of the chicken.

The headless chicken would then flop around for a long time, jumping and rolling, and to me it was not a pretty thing to watch. But it was an ordinary sight in our lives and not watching was counted a weakness.

My father would always have a wash tub handy when he killed a chicken and he'd drop the tub upside down over the headless bird so it wouldn't get up under the house, or flop off where the dogs could grab it.

In answer to the question Suzy O. asked, yes, I chopped off the head of a chicken, once in my life. I didn't enjoy it but I never learned to wring the head off like my father did. One time when he was gone I had to kill a chicken, so I used the hatchet.

A lot of people chopped off poultry heads, at the time I'm talking about. Not just country folks, either.

I remember families who'd buy a turkey poult and keep it in a coop for weeks and fatten it up and kill it for Thanksgiving. My family tried that once, but my sister fell in love with the turkey and gave it a name and tied a ribbon on it and wouldn't let it be killed.

What you did after you beheaded a chicken at home, you doused it in boiling water and that made the feathers come off easier. Sort of like scalding a killed hog in a barrel, so its hair could be scraped off.

I don't know whether it would now do little children any good, or harm, to watch the slaughter of animals they eat. But to me it does seem reasonable to teach them that the bacon they have for breakfast comes from a hog, instead of just a supermarket. ❧

I've Been There

One of the customers asked me the other day if I ever watch a certain travel show on TV. I told him I used to watch it but I quit because it never showed any of the places I'd been.

He said, "You mean when you watch a travel program you want to see places you've already visited? Isn't that sort of weird?"

Maybe so but that's about right. Grand landscapes and quaint scenes in distant places don't much interest me unless I'm already familiar with them. I don't understand this curiosity but I have to live with it.

Let me demonstrate. One time I was clicking channels and suddenly I was looking at the courthouse square in my old hometown. I don't know why that place was being shown on television because there's nothing really distinctive about its appearance.

But as long as the camera kept pointing at the courthouse square, I stayed glued to the set. Most interesting thing I've seen on TV in decades. Look, there's the Corner Drugstore where I jerked soda when I was in high school, and there's the barber shop next door, and the picture show, and across the street, just this side of the hotel, is the old Western Union office where I delivered telegrams on my bicycle and kept the floors swept.

The scene didn't stay on the screen but a few seconds and I was disappointed. I'd have sat and watched all day if the camera had roamed every street in that little town and showed every house and every tree and every stray dog. Because I'd been there, and walked those streets and known the people who lived in the houses.

You can show me pictures of towering mountains in Asia and rain forests in South America and smoking volcanoes in Hawaii but I won't find them half as interesting as those dusty streets in that little West Texas town.

I'm married to a person who's the same way. Not about dusty streets in country towns, but about other places she's been.

One night she called me to the TV to see a street scene in London because in one of her previous lives she had lived there, or gone to school maybe, or whatever. I wasn't much interested because I hadn't found her at that time and had never walked on that street.

However. Let's suppose we see a travel program showing London's Sloane Square. I'll be an alert viewer, ready to contribute comments and interpretations. Because when we both went to London that time, we stayed in the funny place just off the square and it had those loud-flushing johns and you could hear them all over the building, even when one exploded four stories up at 3 A.M.

And look, there's the pub where I got the red McEwan's Export bar towel that's on the workbench in the garage.

Not long ago I came across a program showing the Grand Canyon. I like Grand Canyon scenery because I've been there. My partner wasn't at home at the time but if she had been I'd have called her to look at the sundown scene.

Almost all my life I've seen pictures of the sun doing its show on the Grand Canyon but I never was all that crazy about them until I went

93

there. Now I'll study any Grand Canyon picture, a still or a movie, to see if I can see a place I especially remember.

The sundown scene out there must have been more than twenty years ago, when we took the big tour to the West.

Hey, look there. There's the very place we stood that evening, when the sun was doing down and creating all those fantastic colors on the cliffs, and the woman from Pennsylvania messed up the experience for us.

She stood with her back to the canyon, while one of the most extraordinary scenes in nature was taking place, and for half an hour spoke to a friend in a loud voice about the scholastic history of her son, from the time he was in first grade until he entered medical school. Remember that?

The last travel program I watched was shot on the coast of Normandy. I've been there, and I liked the show pretty well because, while I'm not certain, I thought I got a glimpse of the restaurant where I ate sea snails for the first time (ugh), and the lady at the next table had a red dog with her and she fed half her meal to that dog. Which was something I've never seen in America.   ∾

Shhhh!

*A*lmost everybody who plays it agrees that golf is a strange game. Even the rules that govern the behavior of the spectators are strange.

Not long ago I was watching a tournament, and Tiger Woods got really upset because somebody in the gallery clicked the shutter on a camera just as Tiger was about to hit the ball.

He scolded the taker of the picture. Told him to "watch that camera" and I suppose the picture taker felt truly chastised, receiving public criticism that way from the world's greatest golfer.

It seems curious to me that those who stage golf tournaments charge fans admission and then expect them to remain perfectly silent when a player pulls a club back to strike the ball.

I thought of that when I was watching a baseball game the other evening. Here was a guy at the plate with two strikes against him. If he gets a base hit, the runners at second and third come in and win the game. If he fans, the game is lost.

This is a tense situation and a batter must concentrate, think about whether he'll get a fast ball or a change-up or a slider or a sinker or whatever. Are the fans silent, so he can focus on this difficult task?

Why no, 40,000 of them are yelling at him in the hope that he'll get flustered, swing at a bad pitch and strike out. Furthermore, some are shouting insults at him, telling him he's nothing but a bum and has no business in the major leagues.

Now, both the golfer and the batter are up there to swing a stick and hit a ball. The batter is expected to hit a ball coming at him at maybe ninety mph, and he doesn't know whether it'll be high, low, inside or outside. It might even hit him in the head and send him to the hospital.

The golfer's assignment is to swing a stick and strike a ball that's perfectly still, and is sometimes perched on top of a tee to make it easier to hit.

Yet the fans are required to be silent so the golfer can concentrate.

Let's go to basketball. Here's a player at the free throw line, with a chance to win a game if he can shoot the ball up there and make it go in the hoop. This is not easy, as you know if you ever tried it.

It wouldn't be easy even if the basketball player was accorded the respect and silence that the golfer gets. But what he gets instead is a gang of wild-eyed fans just behind the goal, shouting and waving long skinny balloons to distract him.

Then football, oh Lordy. Can you imagine football fans sitting in silence so players can concentrate? Football fans and their noise often become part of a team's strategy, to create bedlam so the opposing quarterback's signals can't be heard by his teammates.

What other sport demands silence from fans? Well, tennis, I guess, at least during serves. But noise is a part of most games we play or pay to see. And I'm here to bet the reason golfers demand silence before they swing is that golf is of foreign origin. Tennis, as well.

If Americans had invented golf, I bet we'd have razzing spectators the same as we have in baseball and football and all the others.

It might be interesting.

Let's say you have David Duval on the eighteenth green and he's all square with Davis Love and he needs to sink a knee-knocking eight-foot putt for a birdie that'll win a tournament with a half-million bucks waiting for the winner. Pressure deluxe.

He stalks the putt. Squats to get the line. Addresses the ball. Takes a couple of practice strokes. Just before he putts, a gang of Davis Love fans directly in front of him start waving towels and yelling:

"You're gonna choke, Duval! It's gonna break right! It's gonna break left! You never made a pressure putt in your life! Choke! Choke!"

If he walks away from the putt and waits, the razzing from the Love fans will just get louder and more insulting. And eventually Duval will have to attempt the putt, with all that racket going on.

And if he sinks it, wow, that'll be an American-style victory. Something like the slugger in baseball who puts one in the seats to win the game, with those 40,000 fans screaming for him to swing at a bad pitch and strike out.   ∾

All Worked Up

Apparently I once had a piece in the paper about a kind of sandlot baseball game called work-up. Because every two or three years somebody writes and urges me to reprint what I wrote about this work-up game.

I don't recall writing about it but I sure remember the game, and learned valuable things from playing it. We didn't call it work-up, though. We called it scrub. Maybe it's still played and I just don't see it.

The best scrub game I ever knew was played on the high school grounds back in my little hometown in West Texas. It was played every day of decent weather, during the lunch hour.

Dozens of players took part, because there were no teams. It was everybody for himself.

The infield of a scrub game looked normal. I mean you had a pitcher and a catcher. First, second and third bases were manned. And you had a shortstop.

But the outfield was heavily populated. You might have forty out-fielders, and they would range from sixth-graders to high school seniors, and sometimes you'd even find a couple of grinning teachers out there, hoping to catch a fly ball.

Because if you caught a fly ball you got to trot in and bat. That was the object—to be at bat.

The other way to get at bat was work up. If a batter grounded out to first, the catcher moved in and got to bat. The pitcher moved to catcher. The first baseman became the pitcher, the second baseman became the first baseman, and so on around.

I was able to see, early along, that working up was way too slow. The only time I ever tried it, I worked up to first base and the bell rang and we had to quit and go in to class.

A far better way was to catch a fly in the outfield.

A glove? No, we didn't have gloves. The ball was what we called an in-door ball, for a reason I never understood. It was bigger than the standard softball we know now, and the early balls of this type had raised rawhide seams that could tear your fingernails off.

I've still got peculiar nails on both hands from catching one of these indoor balls. This ball would get soft with use but a new one was hard as any baseball ever hit out of Yankee Stadium and it was caught barehanded.

One of the great joys of life then was to walk into the outfield, ten minutes before the bell, and catch a fly and go to bat, ahead of all those players who had spent the entire lunch hour trying to work up.

Pitches were slow and most of the batters were right-handed and so left field was often so crowded you couldn't find a place to stand. When a high fly was hit to left, you'd have half a dozen big old 6-foot senior and junior football players gathered under it, to fight for the catch.

By the time I was in seventh grade I had learned something from this situation. I quit trying to get under a fly ball because all those bigger guys would bunch in the same place and knock me down.

So I began standing off to the side, and staying alert. When the big boys all leaped at once to try to catch the fly, often the ball would bounce off their hands and if I was standing in the right place I could make an easy catch before the ball hit the ground. And go on to bat ahead of the big boys who had been knocking me around.

I discovered, later on, that this system often works in other competitive actions, that don't have anything to do with sport. Sometimes, instead of barging into the middle of the action where you are outnumbered and have no chance, it's better to stand a little way outside the fray and catch the balls that fly out of the fight. ∾

#$!!&$#@!!

The other morning as I was leaving the drugstore I walked past the parked car of a woman just as she had a small accident.

What happened was that she dropped her purse, which was one of these roomy jobs with all her stuff loose in there, and several items came flipping out and skittered onto the asphalt of the parking lot. Some of them bounced under her car.

What made this an event to me was that when the purse fell, the woman let fly a spring of astonishing profanity. I mean these were words you might hear at a stag barbecue, so they were really impressive coming out of that attractive woman.

Understand I'm not criticizing. I'm just observing. Maybe this person was already having a bad day by 10:30 A.M. Maybe she hadn't slept well. Her husband was a grouch at breakfast. The dog wet on her new carpet. Her kids were contentious.

Are there those among us who have not lived through such a day, when merely dropping a purse would make us want to shout blasphemy?

That scene made me thoughtful about profanity. We don't see very much in print about the subject, but in my experience its use is spreading. I know those who will argue that using expletives is therapeutic, a way of relieving pressure. Maybe they're right, but this is a sensitive matter, and I don't want to sound like I'm recommending it.

Long ago in our town there was a newspaper columnist named George Bailey. He once dealt briefly with this matter when he was writing about the Chinese. He had found out there is no such thing as a curse word in their language. His comment on that was, "How do they ever put up a stovepipe?"

In some lines of work, profanity is so common that a few workers can't express themselves without it.

In my early years in the newspaper business, I had a managing editor who called me in to talk about an interview story I'd done. The subject was a retired fellow who had spent his life in the oil fields.

My editor wondered why I had not used one direct quotation in the story. He said direct quotations add interest and color and help the reader visualize the subject and understand his character. I told him I didn't use any direct quotes because the man didn't speak a sentence that wasn't loaded with profanity.

That interested my editor and he told me to write the story again and put in direct quotes. So I did, and it was the most extraordinary piece of copy I have ever produced in all my years in this business.

It was a story about the same length as this column and something like every fourth word was unprintable. The man simply wasn't able to express a thought without using obscenities.

When he told of drilling a hole in the ground, the telling was littered with barnyard synonyms for both male and female genitalia, sexual activity of various kinds, and the body wastes of bulls, dogs, horses, and men. He could mention no place or event in the oil patch without preceding it with adjectives suggesting that God had damned it.

The story was not, of course, printed, but the editor seemed fascinated by it and showed it around the newsroom. I still get a little edgy when I think that piece of copy might still be around somewhere in a file. With my name on it.

The late Cayce Moore Sr. of Hearne used to tell a story about his Uncle Dub who had a wide reputation as a champion cusser. When a thing went wrong on the farm, he could spend five minutes cussing about it without ever repeating a phrase.

One day he was driving a team of mules to town with a wagonload of watermelons, and he crossed a shallow creek. Going up the far bank, the tailgate on the wagon fell off and all those melons rolled down the slope and into the creek.

Uncle Dub sat in silence for three, four minutes. His wife, on the wagon seat beside him, held her breath and waited for the storm. It never came. At last she asked if he intended to cuss.

"No," said Uncle Dub, "I don't think I can do it justice."

I thought the woman in the parking lot did fair justice to the dropped purse. I hope things are going better for her today.   ∽

Somebody's Watching

Speaking of car wrecks, I came close to being in a really loud one just the other afternoon.

I was stopped, waiting on a light, at the intersection of Kirby and Westheimer. I was headed south, at about 3 P.M. when busy intersections on weekdays are likely to be quiet, if they ever are.

At that hour most of the long-lunch takers have finally gone back to the office and the early skip-outs haven't skipped out yet. It's a time I like to go to the grocery store or the post office.

So I was sitting at the light and I happened to see this white sedan approaching the intersection from the east, on Westheimer. So he was coming in on my left, and coming fast, which I guess is what got my attention. I mean a lot faster than you expect cars to travel on a city street.

My light turned green and I took my foot off the brake and started to move out and it was like a Voice spoke to me: "Wait. That guy in the white car is not gonna stop for his red light. He's coming too fast."

So I hit the brake. And the Voice was right. The white sedan roared across Kirby without slowing down. Ran the red light and gunned on west toward Lamar High School. I suppose he missed the grill of my pickup probably six feet when he went across.

I'm saying he was more than half a block away when his light went red, so he had plenty of time to see it. He just wasn't figuring on stopping, green light or red or amber.

I needed a few seconds to recover before I moved along again. A driver behind me honked, one of those sarcastic honks that says: "OK, move on out. The light's green and that means go."

So I went, but a few blocks farther along on Kirby I pulled into a supermarket parking lot. And thought a while about what would have come to pass if I'd rolled out in that intersection as soon as my light turned green.

That white car would have plowed into the left front door of my pickup.

One of the reasons I like a pickup is that the seat elevates me a little and I can see better in traffic. Also because I figure in a wreck a truck will give me more protection than I'd get in those squatty station wagons I drove so many years.

But if the white car going sixty had busted my truck on the driver-side door, its nose would have punched two-thirds the way across the front seat.

I can hear the noise of a wreck like that. The thunder of the first god-awful crash. The secondary slam and bang of parts knocked loose to bounce across pavement. The tinkle of shattered glass. And finally the clang of metal parts glancing off curbs.

Then a spooky silence, until the shouts of witnesses begin.

I say sixty mph because it seemed that fast. Maybe he was going fifty, which is still mighty fast on a street like Westheimer. Maybe even forty-five, I don't know. Even at thirty-five we'd both have been wiped out if he'd hit me nose-first in my left-side door.

That little experience has made me thoughtful about the way we go forth daily in this town and bet our very lives that drivers are going to observe traffic lights.

We stop on red and use the waiting time to think about what we're gonna buy at the supermarket, or what we're gonna wear to the party, and when the light goes green we pull on out. It's safe, isn't it? If I've got green the other guy's got red and he'll stop for it.

But sometimes he won't.

The traffic safety people preach to us about waiting, when the light goes green. Look both ways, they say, before we proceed, and wait three seconds.

And if a Voice speaks to you and says stop, listen to it.   ☙

Snake Bit

*Y*ou may remember my Cousin C.T. who gets a mention here some-times. He is the dude I used to follow around on the farm, in the dim past when we were in overalls and clodhoppers. C.T. is the one who put the kitten in a churnful of buttermilk that time, and laid the blame on me.

The summer of 1934 he invented streaking, by running naked all the way from the barn to the grape arbor at two o'clock in the afternoon.

He shared with me his generous store of rural misinformation.

How, for example, if I simply held my breath I could stand bare-footed in a red ant bed without getting stung. This was not true.

How I could chew up a red hot pepper and it wouldn't burn my mouth if I held my nose. This was not true either.

How you could take the sting out of bull nettle by rubbing it in ashes from the cook stove. Again not true.

C.T.'s father had a stock tank where Christian converts from a nearby country church were frequently baptized, to get their sins washed away. C.T. theorized that the tank therefore had to be full of sins, and if you waded out about knee deep you could feel them nipping at your legs. Sure, maybe minnows and tadpoles were doing the nipping but they felt like sins after C.T. had stood on the dam and preached his theory.

The reason Cousin C.T. is in my thoughts now, I had a letter from him the other day in which he asked if I am still going around putting snakes in outhouses.

This is a typical C.T. question. He knows I have never put a snake in an outhouse, or anywhere else. I have always been opposed to associating with serpents. The first snake I ever saw, I turned and went the other way. My policy now is, let snakes alone to do whatever snakes do but I don't want to do it with them.

C.T. was one of these boys who enjoyed the company of snakes. He would catch them and handle them. Let them wrap their coils around his arm. He knew all the kinds, the poisonous and the harmless.

My feeling was, and still is, that no snake is harmless. If you meet up with one without any advance notice, something bad can happen no matter what kind it is. I have proved that this is so.

Up at the old country house in Washington County where my partner and I often hide from city traffic and ringing phones, one time I moved a piece of plywood that was leaning against the house and a small snake was behind the board. It sort of leaped, I'm sure in terror at being disturbed.

I leaped too, and bounced off the corner of the house and dragged my arm through a Will Scarlet antique rose bush which has thorns on it like tiger claws. The snake was a little hognose, which is about as poisonous as a gnat, but I still have the scars I got from meeting up with it.

C.T. was the one who put the snake in the privy, in case I need to tell you. It was a chicken snake he had caught in the henhouse, and it was a good-sized one. I've always felt uncomfortable toward chicken snakes. What I say is, any reptile that can swallow a hen egg whole has got to have a mouth big enough to do you damage.

Three girlfriends were visiting C.T.'s sister this day I'm talking about.

They were in the house drinking iced tea and C.T. figured they would be going out to the privy soon. He put the chicken snake in there and shut the door. We took cover to watch.

What C.T. wanted was to hear the girls scream and come backing out when they saw the snake. Then he would rush forth and catch the thing, let it wrap around his arm, and become a fearless hero.

Two of the girls went to the privy on schedule, stayed a regulation time and came out. No screams.

Two more followed, and the result was the same. No screams. Nothing.

C.T. was crushed. When the coast cleared he went in the outhouse to get his snake. He couldn't find it, and never did.

One person, though, suffered mental anguish due to C.T.'s snake stunt, and that was me. I visited that farm many times afterward and I never went in that outhouse without feeling certain that before I got out I would meet up with a four-foot chicken snake.   ∽

2.

A Little Trip

In September of '03 my partner and I decided to spend a significant amount of money the children thought they were going to inherit. So we got on an airplane and went to Europe and stayed a month.

Flew to London for a few days, and then took a train over into France. Stayed in Paris long enough to gain about four pounds each, and then got a car and drove down to the Dordogne area, east of Bordeaux. We rented a house in the village of Tremolat, on the bank of the Dordogne River, and kerplunk – stayed there two weeks. Our purpose was to get a sense of what it might be like to live in a small European town. This was a splendid experience.

What generated the journey was something that happened to me earlier in the year. I was diagnosed with colon cancer. I had surgery and I'm still here and getting on with life. But a happening of that kind is a wake-up call. It says, "Hey, if you intend to do anything you always wanted to do, you better get on with it now." So we parked the dog and went.

I did a dozen columns for the paper about that trip, too many to include in this collection, but what I'd like to do is take a look back through the notebooks I kept and tell you about a few of the things I like to remember.

In London, for example, I felt certain that before we left that city I'd be struck and killed by an automobile while crossing the street. Even so, I love that city, and if I had to leave Houston and live in another metropolis, London would be my choice.

Why? Because anything I'd ever want to buy or see or do is available there. London even has Mexican restaurants serving enchiladas. But what I admire about it the most is that its people know the secret of living together in a crowded space, and that secret is, be nice to one another. This was my third trip to London and I've not yet met an unpleasant person there, and yes, I'm counting hotel clerks and taxi drivers.

The best thing that happened to us in London was that we were taken in as houseguests by Wendy and Christopher Matthew. In one of her former lives, when my partner lived in England and attended London School of Economics, Wendy Matthew was one of her roommates and they have maintained a Trans-Atlantic friendship ever since.

The Matthews have two grown sons and I almost got my fill of hearing that family talk. I happen to love hearing English people speak. My favorite speaking voice on this planet belongs to Diana Rigg, the lady on that PBS program, *Mystery*. Well, Wendy Matthew talks almost exactly like Diana Rigg. I count it an entertainment just to hear her tell how to make a blackberry crumble, or talk about what the family dog did last night. (That animal may be unique. He's a kerry blue terrier who has decided to be a watch dog in reverse. He gives a welcome wag to visitors entering the house, but he doesn't like them to leave. He's been known to bite a person leaving the Matthew home against his wishes.)

Paris? Well, I almost missed Paris because we didn't stay long. Long enough, though, to eat way too much, and learn how to get around on the subway, which seemed to me a fine transportation system. (It runs on rubber tires. How about that?)

One of the reasons we went to France was to see how a couple of American tourists would be treated by the French people. When we were there, a great lot of anti-French sentiment was broiling throughout the United States, because of France's refusal to support our war against Iraq. But if the French attitude toward Americans has changed on account of that war, I didn't experience any hint of it. If anybody in France levelled an anti-American remark at me I didn't understand it.

Of course I am not even close to the ballpark when it comes to speaking or understanding French. I can say good morning and good evening and please and thank you and bring me the check, and that's about my limit, but I couldn't see that anybody in France cared as long as I could pay my bills.

An interesting thing about the French tongue is that some consonants are not sounded in pronunciation. For instance, there is no *h* sound, which changes the pronunciation of my last name. It comes out something like Ahl. A hotel clerk searching the computer for my reservation said, "Ah, Monsieur Ahl," and I didn't know he meant me. Your name may change when you travel. In Mexico I was Señor Holly. I wonder who I would be in China, or Egypt.

The pronunciation of Tremolat, the French village where we rented the house, is TREM-uh-lah, with the *t* silent. When we were both a good deal younger, we were on one of those hurry-or-you'll-miss-Switzerland tours of Europe where you visit two countries per day, and we spent one night in Tremolat and we loved the place. Spring was in bloom then. Larks were singing in the fields and the light was soft and church bells were chiming and the air was fragrant with the flavors of life. We hated to leave.

We said, "One of these days, we'll come back, and rent a little house, and stay for a while, and try to learn how it feels to live here." So that's why we went back to Tremolat, a village of about five hundred people. It has one hotel, one bakery, one grocer, one school, one bar, two restaurants and a beauty parlor.

The buildings are of stone, almost all with red roofs.

Within a block of the city hall we rented a house that's probably three hundred years old, but a renovation gives it a functional kitchen and a bath and a half. Chickens belonging to the neighbors clucked and scratched in our back yard. We gathered ripe peaches and walnuts that fell from trees that brushed our walls. We bought fresh vegetables and eggs from smiling farmers who offered their produce in the village square. We cooked and washed and hung clothes to dry in the back yard. Mornings and evenings we strolled and nodded and said our *bonjours* and *bonsoirs* to the other strollers, and everyone was so polite and the village calm and peaceful.

And so there at Tremolat we had our little two-week experience at European village living. It was a fine adventure, and at times we began to feel settled and homey. But of course we weren't trying to fool anyone, and we didn't. The French can spot Americans before we ever get out of our rent cars. It's as if we carry signs, or give off a scent detectable from a hundred yards.

A pleasant surprise for me was the telephone in the old house we rented. It was an extension line off the phone of our landlord next door. I had grave doubts about that phone because this was a working trip for me, and when I finished a column I would need to plug my portable computer into a phone and try to send my day's work to the *Chronicle* in Houston. But that little Mickey Mouse-type phone was a sweetheart. I hooked it up, dialed the *Chronicle* direct, and my stuff zipped across the Atlantic without a hitch. In two weeks that connection didn't fail me once, as long as I could time my use of the phone when the landlord's teenage daughter wasn't on it.

That may not seem extraordinary to you, but to me it was because it hasn't been long since I was having trouble transmitting the column to the *Chronicle* from my home inside Houston's Loop 610.

Shortly after we arrived in Tremolat we had a brief visit with our landlord, Andrew Calvert, that demontrated how small the world has become because of the Internet. Calvert is British, which I appreciated since my French is non-existent.

Our second day in town I wrote a piece about Tremolat, about where it was, and why my partner and I were there. Sent it to Houston, where it appeared in the *Chronicle* a few hours after I wrote it. It was published nowhere else. That morning Calvert came over to see if we were getting settled in, and I mentioned to him that I had written a column about the village and people in Texas might be reading about it that day. And he said, "I know. The mayor brought me a copy of it before breakfast."

My guess is that every morning, having his breakfast coffee, the mayor boots up and checks the Internet for anything new that might be posted about his village.

Checking my notebooks, I see that I did experience one disappointment on this trip. We'd driven from Tremolat to the neighboring town of Le Bugue, for groceries at a modern supermarket there. The store was great. I especially admired the way fresh fish was displayed, laid out so the customer could lean in and sniff it. We bought some beautiful Dover sole for about $7 a pound. But I thought the prices for sirloin and T-bones were pretty steep. I was drawn to a sign that advertised cheval filet for $10 a pound. That's horse meat, which I understand is popular fare for many Europeans.

I tried to get my partner to buy a chunk, so I could write a column about having horse meat stew. But she wouldn't do it. ∾

He's Feeling Chatty

Everybody I know complains about telephone cold calls, like late in the day when you're enjoying your toddy or your supper and a person calls wanting you to buy something.

Such calls can be irritating but sometimes I don't mind them if I'm lonesome or need a break from whatever I'm doing.

An example: At about two o'clock in the afternoon I had a call and I was glad to hear the phone ring because the morning had been quiet and I was looking for an interruption.

Since 8 A.M. I'd been working on a piece for the paper that wasn't turning out right. In fact I thought it was nothing but a clunker and what I wanted to do was hit the delete button on this machine and send that stuff into the wild gray nowhere.

But I couldn't do that for obvious reasons, the main one being a 5:30 deadline I had to make if I want to keep getting paid. So the ring was welcome. Sometimes a short break will unclog the brain and make things work better.

The call was from a woman with a pleasant tone. She wanted me to make changes in my telephone arrangement and was offering a deal. Without any casual ado she began her little spiel.

I apologized for interrupting and asked where she was.

The question seemed to puzzle her. "You mean, where am I?"

Yeah. Was she in Houston? In Texas? I like to know where people are when I talk to them. It helps me see them.

She said she was in Louisiana. In Lake Charles, I think. Maybe it was Lafayette. I didn't take notes because I had no idea I was going to write about this at the time. I was just talking on the telephone.

I asked if she was at home, or in an office.

An office, she said, and went back to her sales spiel. I could tell she was reading it. I hate it when they read their pitch that way. To begin with, it's poor salesmanship. When they're trying to sell stuff on the phone, seems to me the least they can do is memorize the pitch and present it in conversational style.

Me, I never buy anything on the phone from people I don't know but even if I did I wouldn't buy it if they had to read their sales talk.

When she finished reading I asked what her name is.

"I beg your pardon?" she said.

So I repeated the question, which seemed a reasonable one to me, and yet she reacted as if nobody had ever before asked for her name.

But she recovered and gave her name and it's Phyllis.

I told her I liked that name, that I went to school with a girl named Phyllis. Phyllis Bishop, a nice girl, played basketball, and had a brother they called Jimbo. Lived up there in that South Plains country somewhere. At Matador, I think, or maybe it was Muleshoe.

Phyllis on the phone said she'd never liked her name much, and asked if she could sign me up for the deal she was offering. She seemed to be getting in a hurry for some reason. These people need training in the social graces.

Seeing she was in Louisiana, I wondered if Phyllis ever got over to

Alabama. Told her I've got a grandson in Mobile. Lives right there on the bay. Good kid, too. Junior in high school. Got his head on straight. Makes good grades. Keeps his hair cut. Did Phyllis have grandkids?

She said no, she did not, that all she wanted to know was whether I would sign up for her telephone offer.

I told her not to fret about grandkids. These things take time. Then I asked if she ever got out of that bayou country and drifted up around Shreveport. I've got people there, north of Bossier City. Maybe she's run into that bunch of Hales in that part of the country, up there around Plain Dealing and Bolinger, close to the Arkansas line. My Uncle Bird Hale's got a place up in there. Call him Bird because off and on he's been in the chicken business ever since they invented feathers. You know the Old Woman who lived in the shoe, and had all those kids? Well, Uncle Bird and his wife, call her Myrt, they've got …

Phyllis? Hello, Phyllis? Phyllis? Hello?   ⌒⌒

We All Pay

My Friend Mel came by the house before breakfast and wanted to know if he could borrow a bagel.

On the way from his place to mine I expect he passed half a dozen stores where he could have bought bagels. His problem is not bagels. It's loneliness. His wife, Christina, has been at her sick sister's for the last ten days, and Mel is not really operative without his mate.

We didn't have bagels but I found him some shredded wheat and a ripe banana and he settled in to read the paper and said, "You go on with whatever you're doing there. I won't bother you."

In about three minutes he asked, "What you writing about this morning?"

I told him at the moment I was writing a check to the Internal Revenue Service, and trying to find the form I needed to send in my quarterly payment.

"Son of a gun," he said. "I'm glad you reminded me. With Christina gone I'd forgotten all about that. But don't let me disturb you. Go ahead with your business there."

Another three minutes later he said, "Talking about income taxes? I've got a little situation with taxes that's really bothering me."

Told him I did too. Income taxes have been bothering me ever since my first pay day.

"No, that's not what I mean," he said. "I've got this friend, pretty good friend, too, and he hasn't paid any income tax in about fifteen years."

I've heard about people like that. They've got all these elaborate tax dodges figured out and they whittle their tax payments down to almost nothing. I've never understood how that's done.

"This guy hasn't got any dodges, that I know of. He just doesn't pay taxes."

Not any?

"Not a dime. He doesn't even file a return."

How does he get away with that?

Mel shrugged. "I don't know. I told him he's gonna end up in big trouble and he said maybe so but it hasn't happened yet."

This guy told Mel about being a tax dodger?

"He sure did. He's talked about it two, three times to me. What he did, he moved down here from the Midwest, like Ohio or Illinois or somewhere, and when he got a new address and all, he just decided not to file a tax return, to see what would happen. Says he's against income taxes anyway."

And what did happen?

"Nothing," Mel said, "At least that's what he tells me."

I said that was hard to believe.

"I know. But I think it's true. I figured the guy would get a letter, or a phone call, or maybe some burly person knocking on his door and telling him to straighten up and pay. He says no. Nothing like that's happened."

It will, I said, and it's going to be really bad news. Is this fellow employed? Does he have a job? Does he have taxable income?

Another shrug from Mel. "He's sure not on the streets. He has a nice home, a family. Drives a good car."

I asked how Mel met him.

"He lives in my neighborhood. See him all the time. See him walking his dog. He's just a guy, you know, who doesn't pay taxes, and I don't know what to do about it."

He could just do nothing, couldn't he?

"Yeah, but it's a problem. He seems like a nice fellow and yet, he's cheating, on all of us. He's not paying his way. And I'm paying his part, and you're paying his part, and it tees me off."

I told Mel he could blow the whistle on the guy. Last I heard there was a law about things like that. Report a tax dodger and you get rewarded with part of what he owes.

"I know, but come on, who wants to be a stool pigeon? Think about it. If I call the IRS and say, 'Hey, I've got this neighbor hasn't paid a dollar of income tax in fifteen years.' So they collar him and do whatever they do to people like that, and how'm I gonna feel, rest of my life?"

I could see his point.

"My neighbors would know about it," Mel said, waving his arms. "Everybody would know about it. I'd walk on my own block and people would say, 'There goes the stool pigeon.' I couldn't live with that. This guy's doing wrong but he's still a pretty good fellow and I'd hate to get him in trouble. Tell me, what would you do in my place? Would you squeal on this guy?"

I thought about it for ten seconds and told Mel I probably wouldn't, at that. ❧

My Name's Not Francis

One of the customers has written in to ask if I've talked to any mules lately.

Which is an extraordinary coincidence because it happens that I did, in fact, speak with a mule, maybe on the very day that letter was written.

The mule I talked to recently was standing near the fence on U.S. 281 somewhere between the South Texas towns of George West and Alice. It was a red mule, and really big. That's what stopped me.

Most mules are particular about talking. But through the years I've written quite a lot of favorable stuff about mules, and I suppose for that reason they'll talk to me when they might ignore the general run of tourists.

I'm often challenged by those who question that I actually converse with mules.

And I've not been able to prove that I can, because I can't get a mule to say one word to me if anybody else is within hearing distance. I can't explain this. I suppose it's just the way mules are.

Here's a tip, if you ever want to try getting a mule to talk—start with a compliment. All mules are vain, and easily influenced by praise. I told this one on Highway 281 that the sight of him standing there with the light behind his figure made a mighty spectacular scene.

"Good eye," he said. "Most days I can stand here all day and nobody even waves or looks at me. I'm a special mule. I'm a little better than seventeen hands tall. I don't suppose you know what that means."

I told him I do know a mule thing or two. I know that a hand is four inches and seventeen of them is up there near the top of the scale, for mules.

"Very good," he said, and smiled. A mule smiles with its long ears, by bobbing them gently. "You don't get many mules above seventeen."

I asked how things were going for him and he said, "If I had it any better I'd send for help. The fellow who owns this ranch is so good to me it's embarrassing. I'm a sort of museum piece, I guess. When he has guests he calls me up to the barn and gets me to walk around and look beautiful, and that's about it."

He doesn't have to do any work?

"No way," the mule said. "I wish I did have work. Mules were bred to work and this world is now a better place for labor mules have performed, and I feel my life is being wasted. I could make a difference, a mule like me."

His owner has never even put harness on him, and asked him to pull a load?

"Never," said the mule, shaking his great head, and those ears wobbled from south to north instead of east to west. "And I beg your pardon about that term you used, owner. I'm not owned by anybody. I'm my own mule. Think of it this way. I live on this guy's place in luxury. In winter I have a warm barn to stay in. I have anything I want to eat. If I get sick I'm doctored by expensive vets. Now you tell me, am I owned by this guy, or do I own him?"

I saw he had a point there. He was, then, a completely happy mule?

He raised his head and looked to the north a few moments, and seemed thoughtful. Then said, "Truth is, I'm lonesome, a little. Oh, sure, we have other animals here on the ranch but they're mostly cows. Cows, oh boy."

He doesn't like cows?

"It's not a matter of liking or not liking. It's just that they're simply so dull witted. I mean, come on, a cow's not gonna have a thought about anything beyond a drink of water and a mouthful of grass."

How about horses? Surely a ranch this size will have horses.

"Yeah, well, horses are half a step up from cows, all right," the mule said. "My mother was a horse, you know. She was the sweetest mare in Texas and I loved her dearly. I stayed by her side two years but I never once told her a joke I didn't have to explain the punch line when I finished."

How about his father?

"He was just passing through, you might say, and I never knew him, but from what I've heard from older mules across the highway, he was some kind of a jack. Well, I better get on back toward the barn. They come looking for me if I don't show up for supper."

What I learned from that visit is, one mule per ranch is not enough. I'd say keep two, at least, because a mule needs intellectual stimulation.

It's Really a Simple Game

One of the customers has challenged me to write something about the game of bridge.

I don't play bridge but one time I heard a conversation about it. Never mind who these two people are:

"I'm bored," she said. "Sick of TV. Let's turn that thing off."

And he said, "Why don't we play a card game or something?"

"Honey, the only card games you know are those kid things. I don't want to play Old Maid."

"Teach me to play bridge then," he said.

"It takes four people to play bridge."

"Well, give me a quick lesson and then we'll call Clara and Bob and that makes four."

"You don't learn bridge in one easy lesson. Besides, I hate trying to teach you anything. You argue about every point."

"No I don't."

"Yes you do."

"Come on, give me the lesson. I promise not to argue."

"All right, we'll try. But I know you'll argue."

"No I won't. Why do you have two decks of cards?"

"Because," she said, "in bridge two decks are used."

"I don't see why you'd need two decks," he said.

"See there? You're already arguing."

"No I'm not."

"You are too."

"Am not."

"Are too. But let's get on with it. We'll deal out four hands, face up, so we can talk about them. There. That's your hand. First thing you do is arrange your cards according to suit and count your hand."

"I've counted it. I've got thirteen cards."

"You always get thirteen. Everybody does. What I meant is, you count your hand's value. Like you've got nice spades there. Your ace is worth four points, your king's worth three and your jack one. That's eight points, in spades alone."

"Why is an ace worth four points?" he asked.

"It's just a method of evaluating a card."

"Then what's a four worth? I've got the four of hearts. It's the only heart I've got."

"Then it's a singleton and you count it two points."

"It's a what?"

"A singleton. It's a single card, the only one of a suit, so they call it a singleton."

"Why don't they just call it a single?"

"Honey, look, I did not originate the terminology used in this game. If you like I'll call the International Bridge Council and …"

"Are you being sarcastic?"

"No. Yes. Yes I am."

"You don't have to be sarcastic. Why do they call it contract bridge?"

"The winning bid is the contract," she said. "On this hand, you'd probably be the high bidder at four spades, which is game. That's the contract, and you either make four spades and fulfill the contract or you don't. I think on this hand you wouldn't. You'd go set."

"I'd go what?"

"Set."

"Why would I go set?"

"Because Clara's going to lead from her doubleton and …"

"What's Clara got to do with anything?"

"If Clara and Bob were here, playing partners on this hand, she would lead Bob a club and he's got the ace and king. He'd cash those and then he'd lead her a club back. Do you see why?"

"No."

"Because he figures she's void and can trump."

"Void?" he said. "That sounds obscene."

"It's not obscene. It just means you're out of cards in a certain suit."

"I still think it doesn't sound very nice. What's a trump?"

"Spades. Spades are trumps. When Clara trumps the club and plays her ace of hearts, you're down one. Set, before you ever get in."

"You sound glad."

"I'm not glad. I'm just telling you."

"Well, if that's all there is to this game, I don't know why everybody thinks it's so tough. Can I call Clara and Bob now?"

"Honey, you haven't even heard about bidding yet. You don't even know about trumps."

"Sure I do. Spades are trumps."

"But sometimes they're not. Sometimes they're diamonds. Sometimes they're hearts."

"Then why did you tell me they're spades?"

"Honey?"

"Yeah?"

"Let's play Old Maid."   ❧

Slippery Slope

*S*he came up to me in the parking lot of the supermarket while I was loading my groceries into the pickup and she said, "Do you want to hear a story? Take just a couple of minutes to tell."

Asking me if I want to hear a story is about the same as asking a cat if it wants cream. I told her to go ahead, what's the story?

"To begin with," she said, "I'm not gonna say whether the story is true or not, OK?"

OK, proceed, because the sun is heating up.

"There was this nice old lady, right here in town," she began. "Call her Ms. B. She had a nice house, but she had no family. No husband. No kids. Nobody, except a nephew who lived up in New York.

"Well, Ms. B got sick and weak and couldn't take care of herself, so this nephew came down here and hired a person to live with Ms. B and take care of her. I'll call this person Rose, the one that was hired.

"Ms. B was a sweet old lady, and she wasn't too much trouble to see after. All she did was watch her soaps and game shows and read a little bit, and she didn't eat much, and she was easy to please. This Rose person was paid well, and had a pretty nice deal. She could have company if she wanted to and Ms. B wouldn't ever know anybody else was in the house.

"This nephew in New York never came to see how things were going. He'd call once in a while and talk to Ms. B and she'd say Rose was doing a good job and she was getting everything she needed and all. He'd send money every month for the bills and for Rose's pay, and he'd always tell Rose if Ms. B needed anything extra, why just let him know.

"Well, Rose had this boyfriend, man friend, whatever you'd call him, that came around sometimes, and he was always in a bind for money. Rose took to loaning him fifty bucks here, and seventy-five there, and sometimes a couple of hundred.

"Then he'd start asking for more, like five hundred, that he needed for some kind of deal he had going. Well, Rose didn't have that kind of money to loan, but she had this account that the nephew provided for household expenses and she let the guy have the money out of that. She was sweet on him and couldn't say no.

"Of course he kept wanting more and more. One night he was there and wandering around the house and got into Ms. B's silver. He held up a silver ladle and said, 'You know what I could get for this? Probably a hundred bucks, maybe more.' And he took it.

"He also took knives and forks and other stuff and Rose begged him not to do it, but he'd say, 'Old gal won't ever miss a few pieces of this stuff.'

"Then one night he asked if Ms. B had a safe, where she'd keep jewelry. Rose said no, she kept her jewelry in a drawer right by her bed. He said, 'Tell you what, baby, you get me in that drawer and we'll cut out of here and get married.'

"What Rose did, this is amazing, she gave Ms. B an extra sleeping pill. Knocked that poor old soul out, you couldn't wake her with a brass band, and lover boy came in and took his pick of the jewelry out of that drawer. Two diamond rings that I remember, and a string of pearls.

"My guess is he carried at least $50,000 worth of stuff out of that house, and, of course, he never came back to marry Rose. She's never seen him again.

"Not long after that, Ms. B had a stroke and died and when the nephew came down for the funeral he gave Rose a check for $5,000 and thanked her for doing such a good job of taking care of his auntie. Now what do you think about that?"

What I think is that it's a fairly good story that sounds fishy in places, but I could hear the ring of truth in there somewhere.

One thing for sure, there's no doubt about who Rose was.   ∾

Merle and Me

My friend Merle Haggard has a new album out, titled "If I Could Only Fly." This means a lot of work for me.

It means I've got to go out and buy that album and learn all the words to those songs so I can continue my career of singing with Merle.

We have been a team now since back in the '60s, just a few years after he was released from San Quentin Prison, and over the years we've become pretty close.

No, I don't mean I've actually met Merle Haggard, but I consider him a friend anyway due to all the singing we've done together.

We do it on the road, when I'm rolling down the highway. Nobody in the car but just me and ol' Merle. Me behind the wheel and him on the radio, or on the tape deck.

I wish you could hear us doing "Mama Tried." I think we sound the best together on that number. I like the tempo, and the key is about right for me. You ought to hear us when we take a deep breath and raise our voices and let fly those passionate words, "I turned twenty-one in prison, doin' life without parole …" Man, you ain't heard nothin' if you haven't heard that.

Well, actually there's no way you can hear it. Nobody hears Merle and me, except maybe a few crows sitting on fence posts along the highway. Even so our singing is important, to me at least. I don't know what Merle thinks about it.

I've invested thousands of miles and an ocean of gasoline, learning his songs so I can sing with him while I'm traveling.

The toughest of his numbers, for me, was the one about the train engineer. I can't remember the title now but the lyrics tell about this engineer whose career on the rails is hard on family and normal living, but he can't give up his train.

That song has a lot of tricky lyrics but I finally learned them during a ten-hour trip between Houston and the Big Bend.

Oh, sure I've sung with other performers. Willie Nelson and I sang together a few years but we never hit it off well. I love Willie's songs but that dude is so unpredictable on his phrasing, he's too tough for automobile singers like me.

Listening to Willie is fine, but just try to sing with him and see what happens. He'll leave you out on a limb, singing by yourself. I don't want to sing alone. I won't open my mouth to warble a note unless I can sing with a big star.

Karen Carpenter and I always got along all right. I love her melodic voice and I still grieve that she's gone. Karen and I sounded really well on "Yesterday Once More."

Can you hear us? "When I was young I listened to the ray-dee-oh, while they played my favorite songs. I would always sing along, it made me smile …"

The last few years I've been training my partner to sing in the car, and she's making progress. The training album I've chosen for her is Billy Joel's "The Stranger," which includes several numbers that are not easy.

That "Italian Restaurant" song, for example. There's a tough one. The lyrics have the singer remembering Brenda and Eddie who made a beautiful couple back in the summer of '75. Nobody looked any finer than Brenda and Eddie, driving around with the car top down and the radio on.

In that song Billy Joel recalls the sad story of that couple's marriage and its quick collapse and the lyrics are delivered so fast you've got to be a pretty sharp car singer to memorize the words and keep up with Joel.

But there's nothing better than car singing to melt the miles away during a boring trip on an interstate highway. Not long ago we left San Antonio working on the Italian restaurant song. We kept at it through Seguin, Luling, Schulenburg, Columbus, Sealy, and didn't stop until we got to Katy, and still we didn't have all the words quite right. But when we get it down pat, we'll be a sensation on the road.

I'm about to leave on a little trip up in the East Texas Piney Woods. Time I get back I ought to know the words to a couple of those songs on the new album by my friend Merle. ❧

All Aboard for Palestine

*L*ook here what came in the mail. A letter from Jack Hinton who was mayor of Jewett, Texas, when I was keeping up with him back in the '60s and '70s.

In country towns like Jewett the mayor may stay in office years and years. Much longer than Bob Lanier ever did here in Houston, or even longer than Oscar Holcombe, who kept getting re-elected so many times they named a street for him, and a wide one, at that.

Back when I was traveling all the time, before my stomach rebelled and said I couldn't eat any more barbecue or chicken fried steaks, it seemed like every time I stopped in Jewett the mayor was still Jack Hinton. He always said nobody else wanted the job. Of course he already had a steady job, running the bank. He was president of it, I guess, but I never did ask.

You've probably been through Jewett whether you know it or not. It's right in there between Buffalo and Marquez, on U.S. 79 in Leon County. About forty miles southwest of Palestine, if that helps you any.

I always enjoyed stopping there because Cokey Evans at Jewett Drug had a pea-shelling machine in the back of his store. You could stop along the highway and buy a bushel of blackeyes or purple hulls and take 'em to the drug store and get those babies shelled. A great service. Sort of the same as somebody cleaning your fish for you.

I liked hanging out in that store. Seemed to me it had a beauty shop in the back, along with the pea-shelling machine.

One day I walked in there and saw this sign, displayed beside a beautiful bedspread. Sign explained that a certain local girl was getting married, and this bedspread would be a gift for her.

Beneath the sign was a list of names, people who had contributed money toward this present. Some had given as much as $5 but most just a couple of bucks, and one or two had signed up for half a dollar.

I liked that as a comment on how small towns operate. Jewett had a lot of widows then, and other folks living on a short budget, and they couldn't buy that girl a fancy wedding present. But they could give a dollar or two toward a really special gift. I'll bet you that spread is still in use today, a wedding gift from half the people in town.

But the best day I ever spent in Jewett was when we flagged the train.

I was visiting the mayor at the bank—this must have been in the middle '60s—and he was talking about the advantages of living in his town, the way all mayors do, and he mentioned that Jewett had passenger train service.

Well, I knew Missouri Pacific ran a hotshot passenger train up through East Texas on the way to St. Louis. I'd seen it pass through Jewett, in fact. But it didn't even slow down.

Hinton said yeah but if anybody wanted to get on it, the train would stop. I wondered how the engineer knew when to stop and Hinton said, "We get out there and flag it down."

That idea stirred me up. Flagging a train sounded like something out of the previous century, and I needed to see it. Hinton looked at his watch and said the train wasn't due for another hour and a half. If we could find a passenger, he'd flag the train.

We passed the word and within an hour we'd rounded up eight or ten children who'd never ridden a train. We had one fellow thirty years old, been living beside those railroad tracks all his life and never had boarded a train.

We ended up with about half a school bus load, and as many adults as kids. We walked across the highway and stood in a bunch and waited for the train. You could hear that big sucker chugging and roaring long before it came in sight.

When finally we saw it I thought: That thing's running so fast Hinton will never get it stopped. But he did, and with nothing but a white handkerchief, held over his head with both hands.

So our bunch got aboard and rode forty miles to Palestine and we organized a little motorcade to drive up there and collect the passengers and haul them back home.

It has always pleased me to imagine that this was the last time a passenger train was flagged down to take on passengers. Which is probably not true but I still like to think so. ∾

Better Than Warm Milk

During the morning coffee hour at the drugstore, the subject of insomnia came up and received a considerable lot of attention.

If the gathering there at the soda fountain represented a fair sample of Houston's population, in this town we have a significant problem with sleeping.

I don't have a solution to the problem, but I'm comfortable talking about it because I'm among the victims of this malady. My trouble doesn't have anything to do with going to sleep. But once I get there I sometimes can't stay, and I've spent my share of time staring at the ceiling between 2 and 4 A.M.

However, the sleep trouble I have now is nothing compared to a spell of insomnia that afflicted me back in the 1980s, when I was sleepless in Houston for two years. A great upheaval was going on then in my personal life, and I didn't manage a decent night's sleep the whole time.

Today, following the meeting in the drugstore, I'm in sympathy with sleep-deprived folks so I'll pass along some of the remedies I've tried, in case they might be helpful.

First, sleeping pills. I'm against those. I tried pills and they made me feel strange, and didn't make me sleep, either. I'm generally opposed to pills of all kinds, and don't take them except under orders from my doctor. Sometimes I'm not even sure he's right about pills. I think most pills are way overpriced and unnecessary half the time.

Also I tried the open-eye method, when you try to stay awake rather than go to sleep. Hold your eyes wide open, even when they beg to close. Don't even blink. Theory is that eventually your eyelids will collapse and you'll sail off into dreamland. This never worked for me but it might for you.

Drink a glass of warm milk. I know people who swear by this one but I don't like the taste of warm milk at any time during daylight hours and it gags me at 2 A.M.

Counting sheep, an ancient method. You close your eyes and picture sheep leaping one at a time over a low fence and you count them as they go over. By the time you've tallied a hundred sheep you're supposed to be drowsy and by a hundred and twenty you're snoring. The sheep wouldn't work for me, though. I was always seeing one old ewe that would balk at the fence and refuse to jump, and several others would bunch up behind her and spoil the procession. When the jam dispersed, several would leap over the fence at once and I'd lose count and worry about the total and that kept me awake.

Another system that's effective for a lot of people is, just don't try to sleep. If you're lying there at 1:30 and you're not sleepy, forget it. Get up. Dress. Wash dishes. Read a book. Write letters. Or watch all-night movies on TV. I've been amazed at the kind of films you can find on the cable at 3 A.M. Chihuahua! Such films never have put me to sleep but watching them is better than lying awake in bed. And they're educational.

Eat something you're not supposed to have. This was one of my favorite remedies. Make a big sundae, with two kinds of ice cream and chocolate syrup and chopped nuts. This may not make you sleepy but you won't feel guilty about eating it because it's supposed to be medicinal.

Call a friend and talk at 4 A.M. This needs to be a really good friend.

During my extended spell of insomnia I did a lot of roaming in the night. I learned to love twenty-four-hour supermarkets at 2:30 A.M., when I was often the only customer in the store, wandering among all that wealth, thousands and thousands of dollars worth of beautiful food.

Something to remember is that sleeplessness is probably not as bad for your health as you may think. I stayed awake throughout those two years, except for short naps lasting from a half to two hours. I couldn't see that it hurt me much. I did lose a little weight and went around looking sort of haggard but I managed to get my work done and pay the rent.

Friends ask me sometimes how I was cured of this problem, and I don't know for sure. The only thing different I did was get married again. I'm not certain that was the solution, but afterward I did start sleeping a lot better. Which is fortunate because I'm no longer allowed to go out at 3 A.M. and wander around town.　　　∾

So Long, O.F.

*M*aybe you've already heard that my Old Friend Morgan died.

Early Friday morning I drove down to the little Brazoria County town of Sweeny to attend O.F.'s funeral service. He died last Wednesday in a Veterans Affairs hospital in Floresville.

The name on his birth certificate is Charles Eugene Morgan Jr. He was eighty-four.

The regular customers will remember O.F. as the friend who went along with me to South Texas every March for twenty years, to meet spring. I ought to say that I went along with him, since it was his idea to go meet spring in the first place.

O.F. was a great idea man. He had one of the sharpest, most retentive minds I've known, and was among the best storytellers this state ever produced.

He could also be so bad, especially when he'd enjoyed too many drops. There are people in the Brazosport area, where he lived for a good many years, who won't spend a lot of time grieving the passing of this guy. Because they didn't like his politics.

I didn't always like 'em either. But that's not important to me. O.F. was still among the best friends I ever had.

Do you know how it feels to be glad, or at least relieved, when a good friend dies? I feel that way about O.F.

In March, I went to that Floresville hospital to see him for the last time. It was a wrenching experience.

That old body was ravaged by disease, reduced to bones and papery, discolored skin. Yet his mind was still in running gear, spinning, leaping across the years, recalling events from his boyhood up through breakfast that morning. All out of focus but refusing to quit.

And those pale eyes, clear and glaring and angry about disappointment and injustice and frustration. O.F. was most always vexed about one thing or another.

So I'm glad he's gone. Maybe that racing mind will get some rest.

The last time he was able to go meet spring, we were rolling along U.S. 281 down below Alice and we talked about dying. Old men do that sometimes. O.F. was against the idea but he'd laugh a little and say he'd accepted that it would happen to him since he hadn't been able to figure a way to avoid it. He was already sick then, and on the way down.

Said he intended to give his body to the doctors, to see what they could learn from it. Said it was the only way he could think of to be of any value after he died.

Yeah, but I wonder now what the doctors will learn from that old body, which was already devastated long before O.F. died.

Now if they could download what's in his brain, they'd have something worth saving. It pleases me to imagine, if they could download it, what they would find.

In the early going they'd have to work through tons of trivial stuff, like maybe a hundred songs O.F. could sing, in Spanish. I think that's when he was happiest, singing those songs. All those verses are still in there somewhere.

Then they'd find a ton of theories, serious as sin, on how the world ought to work instead of how it works now.

I loved having a friend like Morgan because his life was so different from mine. When we met in the '50s I was fighting mortgages and car payments, raising kids and mowing grass. And he was a free-wheeling bachelor, living down in Coahuila, running a mining operation for Dow Chemical and having adventures.

His life would have made a novel, and a movie, full of thwarted love and danger. He was in love with a beautiful girl who was killed in a car wreck shortly before they were to be married, and he never took a wife.

And people whose word I trust have told me this: The Mexican underworld for a time had a contract out on Morgan's life, because of the help he gave federal agents in controlling border drug traffic. When he left that job in Coahuila, he never went very deep into Mexico again.

So long, then, to Old Friend Morgan. ∾

Whiskey in Church

$\mathcal{I}$n a gas station I overheard a fellow talking about something that was "about as popular as whiskey in church." That expression kept me grinning for several miles.

Not that the expression is especially clever or original. What gave me the grins is that hearing it made me remember Old Jim, and the misadventure we had out on the West Coast more than fifty years ago.

He was about thirty then, which is why we called him Old Jim. Those of us who shared his duties were like twenty-two and twenty-four—and we thought thirty was ancient. Also, to me he was the original good old boy.

He came out of some little dusty town up in Oklahoma, and he was a printer. Being a printer in those times meant he could set type by hand and run a flatbed press and operate a Linotype. I met him in Santa Monica in 1945 when we were working on a GI newspaper. I would tell you his last name if I could remember it. He would be into his middle eighties, if he's alive.

Late in that year was a good time, a time of celebration. We'd been in that big war and our side had won and it was over. We'd survived it, and done our grieving about the friends who didn't. We were thinking about the future, waiting to be discharged from the Army and start our lives over again.

Old Jim and I got along all right. We talked about starting a little weekly somewhere, in a country town. He knew everything about putting out a newspaper that I didn't know, and I could do the editorial part that he couldn't, or didn't want to. We'd be a good team.

Maybe we would have, too. I think about that sometimes, and how different my life might have been.

But about the whiskey in church:

One Sunday night in October of '45 Jim and I were wandering around the streets of Santa Monica. Jim had a pint of whiskey stuck in the waistband of his khakis. He had about half the content of that bottle inside him already.

He wouldn't drink in bars. "They all put water in their whiskey," he'd say. When he wanted to drink he bought a pint and drank out of the bottle. This was a common custom then among soldiers.

Jim could manage pretty well, drinking that way. It would have put me prone in the gutter. But printers were strong drinkers. Jim was wide and thick and he could ingest extraordinary amounts of liquids and solids of almost any kind and rise the next morning and do his duties.

On this Sunday night in Santa Monica we were roaming, and came to a church. I don't remember its denomination. The congregation was singing a hymn. Jim paused and said he wanted to go in. I told him he better not go to church half drunk. He said he couldn't help it, that he needed to go in.

And we did, with that bottle of whiskey in Jim's waistband. We sat on a back pew, away from everybody, and sang hymns and listened to the sermon.

The disaster came to pass during what churches call the invitational hymn. When we stood to sing, the bottle somehow popped out of Jim's waistband, probably due to the squeeze applied to it as we rose. He grabbed at the bottle and missed. Kicked at it, hoping to trap it with his foot.

He hit it probably at the neck and it went spinning down beneath the pews. I suppose it traveled maybe halfway to the pulpit.

As quick as the benediction was delivered I rushed out, and waited in the street. I wondered if the police had been called.

Jim came forth steady as pyramids and stood near the front door, smiling, as if he had delivered the sermon and was waiting to shake hands with members of the congregation. When everybody was gone he went back in and came out with his bottle.

Not the minister or any member of that church chose to notice that a sinner had dropped a bottle of whiskey during their service.

In November, after that incident, both Jim and I were discharged. I came home to Texas and he went back to Oklahoma. I've not heard a word out of him since. ꙮ

Call Me Fred

For the morning coffee hour I was a visitor in an office where eight people gathered around a table, and somehow the conversation landed on given names.

Among those eight persons, six admitted they did not like the names they were given by their parents. I was among the six.

The other five answer to Wilma, Orville, Edmund, Myra and Fred.

The name in that group that surprised me is Fred. Why would a guy not like Fred? That was my father's name and I've always wished he had passed it along to me. The Fred at the icehouse said he didn't care for the name because he got it from an uncle he didn't like.

Wilma had a similar story. She was named for a close friend of her mother's who turned out to be not a very nice person.

Orville and Edmund couldn't give specific reasons why they're dissatisfied with their names. Just don't like the sound of them.

Myra said when she was eight years old she began grieving because her name was not Marilyn, as in Marilyn Monroe, and she still yearns to be called Marilyn and not Myra.

I wonder how many people in the world are stuck with names they don't like. Must be millions. Maybe we ought not to name children until they get old enough to pick names they prefer. Parents are always messing up on names.

My mother's first name was Leona, which she didn't care for. She answered all her life only to her middle name which was May. Then when I was born, what did she do? Knocked a letter off the end of the name she didn't like and gave what was left to me.

I don't really hate the name because along with the four-letter family name it makes a snappy byline. Even so, if I'd been doing the picking I wouldn't have picked what I got.

But I've never complained very much because that is not the worst thing they did to me. They gave me a girl's name in addition. It's Carol, spelled just that feminine way on my birth certificate.

For twenty-one years I kept that a secret. If anybody asked if I had a name other than the one I used, I lied. I said no.

Then I went in the Army to attend World War II and discovered that Carol was on my birth certificate as my first name instead of a middle one. And all during that long war, I was Carol L. Hale and there was nothing I could do about it. If I wanted to get my pay, I had to sign the payroll that way.

I did hate that name, with a high-voltage passion, and swore the first thing I'd do when I got out of the Army was go to court and get it off my birth certificate.

But I never have done it, and the other five people there at the icehouse haven't either. Wilma said she didn't do it because it would have hurt her mother's feelings. Orville said he'd thought about it but didn't know how to get it done.

You may remember Johnny Cash and his song, *A Boy Named Sue.* I heard that song well, because I've been there, and known others who have too. I went to school with a fellow named Gladys. It was a family name and he got it for a first one, and I think it was a cruel thing to do to a tiny baby in the crib.

Sometimes names create unexpected difficulty. I was telling the group at the coffee table about a long-time friend with the first name Macon. I always liked the name, thought it was distinctive. But he says it has given him eternal trouble.

"Nobody understands it," he says. "Nobody remembers it. I'm called Malcolm, Nathan, Mallon, Merlon, Manny, Jason, Marcus, Norman. And even Moron. Little kids call me Bacon and fall over laughing."

For a while he tried saying, "Macon, like the name of the town in Georgia." And people began calling him George.

That Georgia city once generated media attention by acquiring a franchise in the Central Hockey League and naming its team Macon Whoopee. (Yes, really.) My friend's wife said he ought to get a Macon Whoopee T-shirt and when he introduced himself he could point to his name on the shirt.

"I told her no thanks," he says. "Pretty soon they'd be calling me Whoopee. I'll stick with Malcolm and Nathan."

But here's what the folks at the icehouse found the most interesting: When my friend and his wife had a son, guess what they named him. Yeah, Macon. ❧

Bombs Away

$\mathcal{H}$ere is a letter from my Cousin C.T., who may be remembered by the regular customers. C.T. is now retired and living his life all over again and finding, as he says, that he likes it better the second time than he did the first.

The way he does this, he sits in his big soft chair and reviews all the significant events in his experience, and fills in certain details that were missing when these events took place.

In this letter he asks, "Do you remember the time we camped on the Colorado and catapulted the rancher's kid into the river off a willow tree?"

That question is a fair example of C.T.'s custom of filling in details. But yes, the occasion he refers to is firm in my memory.

Along about this time of year, a little gang of us in the old hometown would go fishing and camping at a place we knew on the Colorado River. Somebody would get the use of a car, or an old pickup, and we'd stack our gear and ourselves in that vehicle and go to the river four or five days.

This was on the Upper Colorado, close to Goldthwaite in Mills County. Some person in one of our families knew a rancher who would let us come through his place to get to the river, and this was a fine place to camp.

Huge pecan and cottonwood and sycamore trees lined the Colorado there and threw good shade in the middle of the day. We seined for crawdads and red horse minnows and set trot lines and throw lines and caught catfish to cook.

We could get eggs cheap from the rancher's wife and somebody among us—we were just a gang of high school boys then—somebody had learned to cook well enough that we survived on fried fish and scrambled eggs and pinto beans, and maybe a squirrel stew on the last day.

Most of the fish we caught by running the lines at night, so during the day we just messed around. We'd rig a rope from a high limb of a cottonwood and nail old boards on the trunk to make a sort of ladder. Climb up there, naked as Adam, and swing out over the river and let go and try to do a flip before hitting the water.

This kid that Cousin C.T. mentioned in the letter belonged to the rancher. He'd come down to our camp and stay with us, all day long. At first we counted him a pest but we needed to keep the rancher in a good humor so we put up with the kid.

I want to say he was nine, maybe ten. Spindly little dude. Didn't weigh enough to count. And swim? That kid would outswim ducks. He'd get in the river and go bottom side up and disappear under water for so long we'd get worried about him, and then he'd pop up grinning fifty yards downstream.

We'd fling the kid in the river sometimes. He loved it. Two of us would get hold of him, one on his feet and the other his arms, and swing him back and forth two or three times and let go and see how far we could send him, out in the river.

Quick as he hit the water he'd come paddling back, giggling and wanting us to do it again, do it again.

Back then we had an outdoor game we called riding the willows. Find a willow thicket where the trees grew close and straight, twenty or twenty-five feet tall. Shinny up one of those trees until your weight caused it to bend, and then hold on and ride it to the ground. Tree was springy and wouldn't break. When you got off, tree would spring back vertical.

One of us—sounds like something Cousin C.T. might think of—decided it would be a good thing to use a willow as a catapult. C.T. liked reading about ancient wars when walled cities were bombarded with flaming missiles shot over the walls with catapults.

Since the kid loved so much to be flung in the water, we could ride a big willow down, put him astraddle it, let it go, and see how far out in the river it would send him.

Well, the kid loved the idea. He was ready to fly.

Today I still see that little boy coming off the end of that whipping tree and tumbling seventy-five feet out over the Colorado River.

But I see him only in my imagination. Because somebody among us got cool-headed and pointed out that we might fling that kid clean across the river and land him thirty feet up on the far bank.

So we didn't catapult the kid after all, no matter what Cousin C.T. says in the letter. ∾

What He'd Like To Eat

*I*f you offered me a penny right now for my thoughts, I would have to tell you I'm thinking about chicken and dumplings.

I'm hungry, and it's a long time before my next feeding. I'm sitting here dreaming about what I'd like to eat if I could have what I want.

Chicken and dumplings would be a fine starter. Made the old-fashioned way, with the dumplings flattened by a rolling pin and the chicken cooked so long it's slipping off the bones.

If you can't give me chicken and dumplings I'll take spaghetti and meatballs. I want the meatballs to have that deep nutty flavor that seems mysterious, as if nobody knows where it comes from and the flavor is only in the meatballs of cooks who have been fixing them for fifty years.

Next time I go to an Italian restaurant, that's what I'm having, meat-balls and spaghetti. Do they still offer them? Probably the dish is considered low class now.

I was eating spaghetti forty years before I ever heard of anything called pasta. If I'd seen linguine on a menu I'd have guessed it to be vegetable. And cappelini sounds like somebody who'd be playing second base for the Dodgers. I miss spaghetti.

Something else I want is Swiss steak. I haven't had a bite of Swiss steak in thirty years and I liked it because the steak was always tender. How could it be anything else, since it was cooked so long you could point a fork at the skillet and the meat would fall apart? You had to eat the gravy because that's where the meat went, after all that cooking.

Gravy. Now there's a sweet word. I don't get gravy any longer. Instead I get sauce, made with healthy ingredients. Sometimes I wish for the gravy I knew in 1938, before everything that tastes good became poisonous.

I'm thinking about what we used to call skillet gravy. We ate it on nights when we had steak. Notice that noun—steak, the singular form. We never had plural meat, such as T-bones or sirloins, as people do now. Our steak was one piece of beef for the entire family. Probably a slice of round, which was cut into small pieces. These were pounded on a board to tenderize them and then fried in grease in a big iron skillet.

During the frying little pieces of burnt beef would flake off, and they'd be left in the skillet along with the grease when you took the meat out. To make this gravy you poured in milk and sprinkled in some flour for thickening and peppered it good and stirred it to keep the lumps out.

This is the gravy that fed a family of six or eight people when they had only one thin cut of meat on the table. You got only two or three bites of meat but you didn't complain because there was all that gravy as a backup. You spooned it over your biscuits and it tasted more like meat than the meat did.

Also I'd like a nice batch of deviled eggs. Does anybody still devil eggs? I haven't even seen a deviled egg since I attended my last church picnic.

A skillet of yellow cornbread would be all right, with plenty of Jersey butter.

I'm lonesome for a good hot dog, too. I don't know what's happened to hot dogs. I try to eat one now and it tastes like three separate things—mustard, a weiner, and a cold bun. This is not right. The ingredients of a hot dog ought to blend and become better than the sum of its parts.

The best hot dogs I ever ate were sold at Buff Stadium in the late '40s, before Houston got a major league ball club. I think this dog cost maybe twenty cents and there was something special about the bun. It was warm and soft and yet it held up under whatever you wanted to load it with and you didn't taste separate ingredients. You tasted hot dog. I would give $5 for one of those babies now.

For dessert I would like pecan pie with vanilla ice cream piled on top and drooling down the sides.

Or else two or three Eskimo pies.

Or a banana pudding.

Or a plate of fudge with pecans.

These are the kinds of things I would like. But they aren't what I'll get. On account of this diet I'm on, what I'll get is a green salad with vinaigrette dressing and a modest piece of grilled fish. ‿

Grammar Lesson

*E*ver since I've been in the column-writing dodge, certain of the customers have fussed at me about my grammar. Especially teachers, who have accused me of setting a bad example for their students.

As near as I can tell, getting fussed at has not caused me to change any of my bad habits and I suppose that's unfortunate. At least I've been told that it is.

However, it isn't likely I'll improve very much, if any, after all this time. And I'm not so sure that's bad because I like hearing from the ones who do the fussing, and they do seem to enjoy correcting me.

Some are really clever at writing corrections and I expect they'd be disappointed if all of a sudden my grammar, spelling and sentence structure changed, and became textbook correct. I wouldn't want to deprive them of the pleasure they get out of setting me straight.

On spelling? I've been misspelling the same ten words for forty years.

Readers never see most of them because they get fixed by *Chronicle* copy editors, or by this computer that thinks it's a better speller than I am. It underlines in red every word it considers wrong. I don't always agree with the computer and some days this screen has a lot of red on it.

The computer also considers itself a grammarian and an expert on sentence structure and it's forever objecting to my stuff. I try to ignore it. I consider that to be meddlesome. I've got a regiment of high-paid copy editors rummaging in my prose, and I've got those customers who love to write their clever corrections, so I don't appreciate being edited by a machine that operates off a battery.

My shortcomings in the field of grammar originated during my country rearing, out there in West Texas long ago where people weren't judged on what was in books.

Still, I've always known more grammar than I use in the paper. I don't much like rules, on how people talk, or write out thoughts. It's always seemed to me that the main thing is being understood.

But I confess I inherited from my rural kinfolks a couple of grammar habits that drive the textbook people out of their wits. One was here in the column just the other day, when we had the Texas Quiz. I wrote that O. Henry moved to Austin and "sung in a quartet."

I ought to have said that he "sang" in it.

This drew response from the grammarians who explained to me, for time Number 10,000, that I'm not supposed to write that anybody "sung" a song. I can say that a person "had sung" a song, or that two people "have sung" together or that a hymn "was sung" by the choir. But I mustn't say that one person "sung" a song. Because "sung" is the past participle of the verb "sing" and needs a helper word.

Yes, but the trouble is, everybody I grew up with and went to school with were always talking about songs being sung, and they would say that Marvin sung *Sidewalks of New York,* or that Mary Elizabeth sung a nice version of *Mood Indigo* and I heard that so many times it got in my head and stayed.

A further trouble is, the older I get the deeper in me these boners sink.

And I'm taking on new ones, too, especially in spelling. I'm about to wear out a dictionary, looking up words I could once spell but have trouble with now.

One that really wigs me is the old problem about the difference between "it's" and "its." My third-grade teacher, Mrs. Van Gem, gave me a rule about that. She said when you see "it's," with that apostrophe, think "it is." When you see "its," think of possession, as you might say of a cat, "Its tail is as long as its body."

That rule served me well for many years but the misuse of these two words is now so common, I catch myself thinking that "it's" looks all right even when used incorrectly in place of "its." You see it everywhere, even on tall billboards, and often in the text of advertisements.

Over the years I've done some complaining here about that popular boner. In fact, I have sung that song (hah!) over and over again, and I dread the day I make that mistake myself in print. If I ever do, just try to ignore it. ∾

The Face in the Photo

On Monday I observed Veterans Day in private, at home. I dug out a few of my old World War II photographs and tried to remember names.

One time in college, before WWII, I took a course in basic photography, and I remember a rule the instructor talked about. He said that when you take a photo, even if you think it's not important, you need to save the negative and make some kind of record of where and when the shot was taken and who the people in the picture are.

Because if you don't, it's almost certain you'll end up one day with a bunch of faded prints showing the faces of people whose names you'll yearn to remember.

He was plenty right about that.

Here, for instance, is a bad print of a picture I took on the Isle of Capri in the summer of 1944. Took it while sitting in the dining room of a hotel where our bomber crew had been sent for rest camp.

We were stationed down in the Italian boot, near the city of Lecce.

We'd flown twenty-five missions. Rule of the 15th Air Force at that time was that B-24 crews were required to do fifty missions before they went home. When they were halfway through, they got a few days rest, often on Capri.

I don't remember that we did much resting on that beautiful island, but I do recall why I took this picture.

Maxwell, off a farm in the Midwest, was sitting across the table from me. He was the engineer on our crew. We had been served an Italian dish called ravioli, and neither of us had ever heard of it before.

Maxwell was a grinning, fat-faced fellow, twenty-one or twenty-two then. I think of him often. We were together on the flight deck of a B-24 during a year of combat missions over Europe.

He wanted a picture of himself eating something called ravioli on the Isle of Capri. Wanted to send it to his folks back home. So I raised my little camera and took this shot.

To me, the most interesting thing on the print now is an out-of-focus face in the background. It's the face of a young man at the table next to mine and Maxwell's. I caught him in the picture by accident.

He wasn't a member of our crew but I knew him fairly well. He was killed on the first mission we flew after we left Capri and went back to the war.

I'll go ahead and call him Jimmy. That may have been his name but I'm not certain. Probably I could get somebody to do a search of our old outfit's records and come up with his name, but I don't see much point in doing that, not now.

He was maybe nineteen, because he'd been through his freshman year of college. And he was in love. Man, was he ever in love.

I got acquainted with him because we both spent a lot of time writing letters, on days when the weather was bad and missions were scrubbed. I'd find him in the day room, his head bent low over his letter-writing kit. He was a southpaw, and wrote with his left wrist crooked over the top of the page the way they do.

He was a sharp kid. A reader. He and I swapped a lot of paperbacks. I was twenty-three then and felt old compared to most of the guys in our squadron. But this kid seemed mature. He thought and talked about the future.

That was characteristic of young guys in love, who had girls waiting back home. Sometimes, like Jimmy, they had their entire lives planned. Finishing school. Getting a job. Getting married. Building a house. Having kids.

At the time I was glad I didn't have plans laid out like that. It seemed a temptation to the fates, which love to destroy plans. I felt it was almost foolish for a guy to have his life planned in detail, when he's going up in an airplane three or four days a week and getting shot at. The other guys I remember in our old outfit seldom spoke of the future.

I see Jimmy's eager face in this snapshot and I think, here is a life not lived. If it had been one of the others of us, somehow it wouldn't have seemed so bad.   ∿

The Shiner

Due to a mysterious circumstance, I have been walking around the last few days with a black eye.

And this is a serious shiner. I'm talking about a riot of color, all the way from my right brow to halfway down my jaw. I've seen boxers fight through fifteen rounds and get busted in the eye twenty times and go home looking better.

I haven't had a black eye since October of 1945, when I acquired one in a bar out on the West Coast, in Santa Monica. I got that one for talking when I should have been listening.

That was long ago and so I'd forgotten that the general public has an intense interest in black eyes.

A shiner draws notice. You can break a leg and walk six months on crutches and attract less attention than you'll get by going to the grocery store with a black eye.

People don't care how you broke your leg, but they are sure curious about how you got a black eye.

Maybe that's because a black eye suggests some kind of interesting violence. Like a fist fight. Or physical abuse within a family.

One of my editors at the *Chronicle* tells me that most observers, when they see a black eye on a woman, figure she has been knocked around by her husband. Or her former husband. Or her lover. Or her former lover, who is upset about the guy she is seeing now.

But a black eye on a male generates different thoughts. The most common is that the guy was socked in the eye by another male.

However, an old dude of my age is not very likely to do or say anything to get such a sock, so my black eye is a mystery to observers.

I've been telling quite a few lies about it, since nobody will believe the truth.

In the beginning I said I was hit in the eye by a door knob. I was down on my hands and knees, trying to find a lens that had popped out of my glasses, and somebody opened the door and the knob busted me in the eye.

That story didn't play so I changed it, and said I was walking in Memorial Park and a guy hit a softball and it caught me in the eye.

Next I changed over to a fist fight, which is what I thought everybody wanted. I said I was out walking and came up on a large bad person trying to steal a bicycle from an 8-year-old girl and I tried to stop him. I did bury a fist in his midsection but he was too tough for me and hit me a good one in the eye and gave me this shiner.

When nobody believed that one, I gave up, and began denying I'd been hit in any way. When they asked how I got this shiner, I'd say I was born with it and that it's the natural color of my eye.

Actually a black eye is not black. It starts out pink, and gradually turns to red, and then darkens into what I would call a deep purple and it stays that way two or three days.

Then it gets creative and takes on certain shades of green, and delicate lavender, and a variety of oranges and yellows. Right now mine has progressed to a state in which I can move my head this way and that and produce any color in the spectrum.

A couple of days after I got this black eye I was supposed to make a polite appearance at Moores Opera House on the University of Houston campus and take part in a program.

My partner tried to cover up all my spectacular eye color with her makeup. I went forth feeling like I was wearing some kind of mask. It was weird. Is that what women's faces feel like all the time? I thought if I blinked, my face would crack.

I had a dream in the middle of a recent night. In this dream I was walking along a quiet street, minding my own business, and a dog began following me.

I was not afraid of it because this was a small dog, a short-legged creature not much more than a foot long. It kept making charges at my legs, darting in and out, and I got tired of that so I turned around and kicked at that little scamp.

Apparently I tried actually to launch that kick in my sleep, and it caused me to fall out of bed, and on the way to the floor I hit my eye on the edge of the night stand, and that's how I got this black eye. Nobody believes it, but that's the truth.

What I hate the most is that such a small dog, and one that doesn't even exist, has caused me all this misery.   ॐ

Not in Bartlett's

*Y*ou want to hear a quotation I like?

Then listen to John Rotan talking, the day we sat on his front steps in the woods of Tyler County. He was seventy-three and had heart trouble and was explaining why he left a nursing home and moved way out in the timber, to live alone in a tin-roofed shack on the old Doucette Tram Road:

"I got fussed at, when I moved out of that old folks home. They said, 'Why, you can't live out there in that shack and look after yourself.' I told 'em, 'Well, if I die I might as well die where I want to be.'

"I love it here," Rotan said. "This old place is like heaven to me. I can sit under all these trees and the deer come up and graze around the house, and at night I listen to the wolves howling back up in these woods and sometimes they come in close.

"I listen to the birds, the blue jays and redbirds and the rain crows and bob whites. And the mourning doves, so sad it makes your heart melt. I love to hear that Indian hen (one of the big woodpeckers). I hear hawks whistle, and deer snort, and squirrels bark, and I can hear little foxes out yonder.

"I'm not gonna hear things like that in an old folks home. All I heard there was moans and groans. I'd rather be here."

I found those words in a grubby notebook of mine when I was looking for something else. I wrote them in the notebook more than twenty years ago. The next time I was up in Tyler County I went back to see Rotan but he had died, in that shack he loved.

In an old carpenter's chest I have stacks of notebooks I filled back when I was traveling all the time and listening to people like Rotan, and recording what they had to say.

Those old notebooks are special to me and I haven't been able to throw them out. They ought to be trashed because I'm the only one who can read my scribble, and sometimes I can't read it myself. But now and then when I remember they're there, I get them out and flip the pages and find things that seem worth reading again.

Here's a really old one, dating back to the '50s. I was in Kirvin, one of this state's smallest incorporated cities, population eighty-nine. I was talking to the mayor, O.A. Carter, and I'd asked him how much money was in the city treasury.

He said, "I think there's about $36 in it now."

I like that because it has become a unique statement. No mayor in Texas and maybe not anywhere else can say about his city what Carter said that day.

Then here's a few words that came out of Aunt Lizzie Thornton. I met her in Trinity one day, probably in the early '60s. (I should have done a better job of dating these notebooks.) Aunt Lizzie was eighty-six then. She had never traveled farther from home than to Crockett, twenty-eight miles distant. One of the questions I asked her was, had she ever watched television?

She said, "Saw one once. Didn't like it. That's what's makin' these children so bad, watchin' all that stuff on television."

There's a judgment delivered by an old country woman, at a time when few critics if any had yet spoken a word about TV's negative effect on young people.

About that same time I met Dr. Hugo Weige, who had an office in the little town of Industry. He was a DST, which stands for Doctor of Suggestive Therapy. He told me that he did magnetic healing and absent treatments.

The magnetic healing was like the laying on of hands. When a patient with a disability came to him, he placed his hands on the person's body and his personal electricity passed out of him and into the patient's defective parts and straightened them out.

Yes, but then I asked about those absent treatments and I still think his answer was pretty extraordinary. He said:

"That just means we treat people who aren't here. We can treat a patient just by thinking about him. It's a concentrated thought force. We also treat livestock that way. Horses, cows, mules, ducks, dogs, just about anything."

I haven't looked too hard, but I don't find people saying things like that anymore. ❧

An Uncool Move

Tell you what I'll do. If you're the one who picked up my coffee mug off the railroad tracks, I'll give you twenty bucks to send it back, and no questions asked.

I figure you had a right to take it. Probably it qualified as salvage, lying there along the railroad. But that mug is special to me because it keeps my coffee hot better than any I ever had, and I do miss it.

Maybe you'd like to hear how it happened to be on the tracks. However, if you really have the mug, probably you witnessed the curious event that caused me to lose it.

I was leaving town, headed for the old country place at Winedale. The only cargo I was carrying in the bed of the truck was a thirty-six-quart red and white Igloo cooler.

Coolers of that kind come with a tray that hangs just beneath the lid, to keep its contents from mixing with the ice and going soggy. That's where my mug was riding, along with two turkey sandwiches and three

169

or four green jalapeño peppers, one of which I eat every day. Some people take an aspirin daily, or an Advil. I take a green pepper.

Also in the cooler were a six-pack of Bud Light, a bottle of Toad Hollow Chardonnay, and an unopened bag of crushed ice. Also two liters of Evian water which my partner drinks (I'm convinced) mainly because of her French heritage. I prefer branch water myself. The French have sent us a lot of good stuff but plain water at two bucks a quart is a little more of France than I want to buy. Never mind that now, though.

When I leave our house headed for Winedale I take Shepherd Drive north, to catch the Katy Freeway. So on this day I'm scooting along on Shepherd, past Memorial, past Washington, and it's that late afternoon time when everybody in our town gets in a desperate hurry. There's no reason for it. It's nothing but a bad habit.

All the traffic going north is close, and fast, and when we sail through the light at Washington we get faster. I'm in the curb lane and going faster than I want to go but when you get trapped in traffic that way you better go along with the crowd, or else you become an obstruction and cause trouble.

Between Washington and the Katy on Shepherd we have that double set of railroad tracks and they sit high, on a bump. I hit that bump faster than I should have, to keep from getting run over by whatever's behind me, and the tail of the truck kicks up and in the rear-view I get an instant's glance at my cooler flying out of the bed.

Then in the side-view I take a quarter of a second to watch the cooler tumbling off to my left, its lid open and things coming out, and I figure the vehicle behind me has bumped it over onto the railroad tracks.

I can't stop. I can't turn. I go with the crowd across the Katy and I'm six blocks from the railroad before I can get out of the race and stop and think what I ought to do. Should I even bother to go back? The cooler will probably be destroyed, and everything in it scattered over the railroad.

But I do go back, because of my coffee mug. Maybe it survived. It's ceramic and thick and tough. I once dropped it on the kitchen floor and it didn't break.

I have to park almost a block away, so I need around twenty minutes to return to the scene. The cooler is already gone. So is the six-pack of Bud, and the water from France. I find the remains of one of the sandwiches. I pick up the clear plastic bag that held the ice and the ice is scattered and melting.

Here's the cork of the Toad Hollow, still in the neck of the bottle but the bottle is broken and the wine gone. I grieve a couple of seconds. Toad Hollow is not a bad Chardonnay for the money.

But it's replaceable. My coffee mug is not. A friend gave it to me and it has my initials on the side. I believe the mug survived because if it broke I could find chips and pieces of it along the railroad, and I find none.

This is a long shot, I know, but if you happen to have my coffee mug, the twenty bucks is waiting for you. I regret that the Toad Hollow bottle was broken because you might have enjoyed that wine. ∾

Everybody Loved Molly

"Did I ever tell you about Christina's mother?" asked my friend Mel, who had come by to pick up a wrench I borrowed from him almost a year ago. "She was an amazing person."

Christina is Mel's wife and one of my favorite people. But no, I'd never heard anything about her mother.

"Her name was Molly," Mel said. He took a seat in my red chair, with the wrench in his hand, and seemed prepared to talk quite a while. "Even her own children called her Molly. That seemed so strange to me, at first, kids calling their mother by her first name.

"Christina and I grew up in the same neighborhood, in the same block. I knew her when she was in the third grade, and Tim, that's her younger brother, was just a baby and it seemed weird to hear him calling his mama Molly.

"I don't know the reason for that but somehow Molly was just Molly, to everybody. She was Molly to kids in the neighborhood, and to her grandkids. I never heard anybody call her Mrs. Bentley, or mother, or grandmother.

"She was a small woman, and what you'd call cute, I guess. Not a beauty but perky and friendly. Kind of person that when she waved at you on the street you'd want to stop and watch her, until she went out of sight. People were always saying, 'There goes Molly.'

"I'll bet Molly in all her life never weighed more than ninety pounds. She couldn't have been five feet tall and Joe Bentley, Christina's dad, was something like six-two or six-three. Christina remembers when she was a little girl her dad would pick Molly up, just messing around, you know, and carry her around the house on one arm like she was a baby.

"When Christina was ten years old, Joe got himself killed in a car wreck. Everybody said Molly wouldn't last a year as a widow. They'd make bad jokes about it, about how the men followed Molly home from the cemetery. But she fooled them all and never married again.

"One time Christina asked her why she didn't get married and Molly said, 'I didn't want anybody else raising my children.'

"She ended up raising her own and a lot of others. Kids in the neighborhood got where they'd hang out there at her house, and go in and out like it was home. Molly loved it. She'd feed them, doctor their skinned knees, play games with them.

"Sometimes they'd have a kid didn't want to go home and Molly would have to deliver him with the kid yelling he wanted to stay.

"Neighbors used to tell Molly she ought to start a nursery school or something, seeing she was running one for free. But what she did, to pay the bills, was find ways to work at home. She'd do secretarial work. She'd even cook, like fancy wedding cakes. She finally discovered she was a whiz at ceramics, and ended up selling her stuff and making a pretty good living. But whatever she did, she did it at home so when her kids came in she'd be there.

"Christina always said her mother was more like a sister. One thing was, she was so little. By the time Christina came out of high school she was half a head taller than her mother.

"Lot of Christina's friends, and her brother's, too, hung out in that house so much it must have been as familiar to them as home. Even after they went off to school and came back on holidays they'd head for Molly's place.

"Something I remember that seems so much like Molly, after Christina and I got married and our daughter was born, we took the baby to see Molly as soon as Christina could travel, because we figured she was alone, and lonesome. Well, bless Pat if she didn't have two little kids in the house, staying there.

"Turned out they belonged to a couple in the neighborhood who were having some kind of trouble, and they needed a place to leave those kids a few days until they could get the problem straightened out. So Molly took the children in.

"Christina asked her mother how long the children had been with her and she said not very long. Christina said, 'How long is not very long?' and Molly sort of shrugged and said, 'Oh, I don't know. Five or six months, I guess.'"
                                                              ∾

Mutt

"Want to buy a dog?"

The question, delivered with a wide grin, came from the fellow they call T-Shirt, one of the most regular of the regular customers at the neighborhood icehouse.

He was sitting in the bright sunshine at the picnic table out back. Lying at his feet was a curious creature of various colors, ranging from off-white through tan and gray and brindle to coal black. One eye brown and the other a milky blue, what dog people call a glass eye.

I went along with T-Shirt's game and asked how much he was asking for the dog and he said, "Three bucks. And I'll throw in his collar and leash, six cans of dog food and the box he sleeps in."

It happens I am not in the market just now for a dog but most canine creatures are of interest to me, not counting some of your fuzzy lap dogs with pink ribbons tied in their hair-do. I asked T-Shirt what kind of dog he had there.

"Heinz 57," he said. "His mama was part collie and part beagle, and his daddy was a leopard cow dog which is where he gets that glass eye. His daddy also carried some pit bull blood, and there's a little Lab mixed in there somewhere."

I looked hard but couldn't find any Labrador showing in that creature. Asked what his name was.

"Mutt," T-Shirt said, "but he's not particular what you call him. He'll even answer to Fido, or Rover, but Mutt's his main name."

He nudged the dog in the belly with the toe of his boot and said, "Wake up, Mutt, you got a visitor. This here's one of those writin' men. He might want to do a piece about you for his paper."

Mutt lifted his head and started to rise but changed his mind and flopped back down. I noticed when he wagged at T-Shirt he didn't have much of a tail. Two inches, maybe. He seemed like a dog that needed more tail than that.

"Well," T-Shirt said, "he did have a tail when he started out but he lost most of it some way."

Maybe in a fight?

"No, I doubt that. Mutt ain't much of a fighter. He's more of a lover, and good around little kids, if you've got any of those." He gave the dog another nudge and said, "Come on, Mutt, stand up and let's have a look at you."

Mutt finally made it all the way up and I swear he was stranger up than down. His hind legs looked a good deal longer than his fronts, so his rump seemed elevated. I remarked on that curiosity and T-Shirt said:

"Them long hind legs are one of his special deals. Traits, as you might say. Notice when he walks—come on, Mutt, take you a couple of steps—when he walks he's always goin' downhill that way, so he don't ever get tired like ordinary dogs do."

You understand T-Shirt was not really interested in selling Mutt. The two of them are way too attached, so that separation is beyond question. In public places a man will often ask if you want to buy a dog, when all he wants to do is talk about the one he owns and would never sell.

I have known T-Shirt a long time so I wasn't afraid I'd hurt his feelings by telling him I thought Mutt was just about the ugliest canine I'd ever met, and I've visited with dogs in thirty-six states and several foreign countries and seen dogs that hurt my eyes when I looked at them.

T-Shirt's face brightened when I said that. His response was, "Yeah, but Mutt don't know he's ugly. He thinks he's a beauty. This dog will stand at a mirror and turn and twist like a high school girl before a football game. And he's smart, too."

Smart?

"You bet. Now watch this. He does arithmetic." T-Shirt took a little dog biscuit out of his shirt pocket and Mutt sat up and wiggled what was left of his tail. "All right, Mutt. Tell me what's two plus two."

Mutt answered, "Woof! Woof! Woof!"

T-Shirt nodded and tossed the biscuit to Mutt and said to me, "He only missed the right answer by one, and that's pretty close for a dog just four years old."

Mutt sat at attention, hoping for another biscuit, anticipating and quivering and looking so ugly.

T-Shirt grinned and said, "Ain't he a proposition?"   ∾

September 11, 2001

It was a Tuesday morning. I was in the second week of a vacation I'd taken, so I could help with the moving.

We had half a dozen packers in the house, husky guys sent by the moving company to wrap everything breakable and stow it in boxes.

An emotional time, already, moving out of a home you love, leaving good neighbors, going to a new place where you're not certain you'll be satisfied.

I was back in my home office, wrapping my good old IBM Selectric typewriter to go into storage. The feeling was on me that probably I'd never use that fine machine again. So my spirit wasn't exactly soaring when my daughter called and said turn on the television, that something bad had happened in New York City. An airplane had hit a tall building.

My partner has a son in Manhattan so we pay attention to what happens up there.

My first thought was about the day years ago when the B-25 bomber plowed into the Empire State Building, and that was a very bad thing indeed. People were killed and a lot of damage was done. Don't tell me that sort of thing has happened again.

The packers from the moving company were about to disconnect the TV and carry it out. We stopped them and switched on the set and for the next several minutes I was mired in a sense of disbelief.

Come on, could that great World Trade Center building really be burning and were people actually leaping to their death from the top floors? Could this be some kind of sensational stunt? A TV version of Orson Welles' famous radio trick, back in the '30s when he had us believing the country was under attack by Martian invaders?

I didn't see the first building collapse, on what they call live TV. For some forgotten reason I had turned away but I heard a reporter make the incredible statement that the tower had disappeared. That it was there, and burning, and then in the next few seconds it was gone.

Wait a minute now. A 110-story building disappearing?

Then they showed the replay of the structure falling inside itself. For an instant, I actually couldn't accept what I was seeing as factual. It was too much like a *Towering Inferno*-type movie. Thrilling special effects showing tall buildings burning, collapsing, people running in the streets from bulging clouds of smoke and debris.

Realization came soon enough that the scene was factual.

I wonder if there's an adult citizen of this country who hasn't seen moving pictures of those buildings falling, and understood what they meant.

Back in my traveling time I went into some plenty remote places where people had never read a newspaper or heard a radio or seen TV or traveled more than twenty miles from home. But that was twenty-five and thirty years ago and I doubt such people could be found now. Been a long time since I've gone back in the bushes far enough to find a shack without a TV antenna poking out of the roof.

It may be that those chilling September 11 images were seen by more Americans than witnessed any other significant event in the life of this country. That ought to teach a lesson of great value, about our national vulnerability. It can happen here in the continental U.S, despite that it didn't happen in World War I or II or during Korea or Vietnam.

My personal reaction to 9/11 has come in stages.

First, disbelief.

Then shock, at the realization that we have, at last, been attacked by an enemy who would like to wipe us off the map.

Then frustration, because here we are at war, according to President Bush, and yet we don't quite know how to fight back since we don't really know who the enemy is or where to find him.

Then finally came the uncomfortable notion that many of us were overreacting, and the terrorists were winning because our fear of more attacks was limiting our lives. People refusing to fly, or even to ride a bus or a train or make plans. Or have anything to do with a neighbor who has dark skin and looks like a Middle Easterner. Come on, that's pretty ridiculous.

September 11 was tragic, for sure. I don't think we ought to sit in a corner and tremble, though. I suspect terrorism will threaten us for a long time, but it's no more than two-thirds of the world has lived with for generations.   ∾

Their Tree, Their Way

My daughter has recently moved, and we now live in the same town for the first time since she left home in 1970. So I can drive over and see her. Just drop in, like an ordinary father. I like that.

I was sitting in her house the other evening, admiring the Christmas tree with its pretty blinking lights, and I got the grins, remembering the time she and her brother did the Christmas decorating at our house.

They were eleven and nine that year, or close to that, so we're talking about the early '60s. Not that the year matters. Anyway, we decided that since so much of what we do at Christmas is for children, we ought to let the children set the scene.

I should say that I made that decision, not we. Their mother rolled her eyes, said "good grief" and walked away.

The deal was that the kids could buy the tree they wanted and the stuff to decorate it, if they kept inside a reasonable budget. They would

181

do all the work, and their parents would not step in and oversee or criticize.

I was pleased that they were enthusiastic about the project, since neither of them had ever shown an interest in doing around the house anything that resembled work.

My feeling was that they would do a good job, that the responsibility would be a challenge for them. Their mother heard me say that and repeated her previous comment: "Good grief."

We lived just a block from a shopping center then, so that's where they went for the stuff. They came home with a Christmas tree in a box. It was a fake tree. Its limbs were metal. So was its trunk, which had holes where the limbs were intended to fit. Its foliage was shredded plastic in glittery colors.

I believe it was the ugliest object I've ever seen.

In addition to that dreadful tree, they had bought a color wheel with an electric motor. They set the color wheel in the middle of the living room, on top of a cardboard box that once held a six-month supply of cat food.

At night when the color wheel turned, it cast floods of light on the glittery foliage of the tree. Red for a second or two. Then green. Then white.

This produced an extraordinary effect because the predominant fixed color on the glittery branches was purple. Your favorite Christmas color, right? Purple. I thought when the wheel made its cycle, bouncing red and green rays off those purple limbs, the observer was looking at what a serious hangover feels like.

That subdivision we lived in then was fairly new, and all its houses had one thing in common—a large picture window at the front. This is where homeowners put their Christmas trees so they couldn't be missed by drivers-by.

Nobody ever mentioned it, but these trees were located and decorated in the true competitive spirit of Christmas. My tree is prettier than your tree, and bigger as well.

Our kids loved their fake tree. They bicycled around the neighborhood and returned with the news that nobody had a tree anything like theirs, and this was certainly true.

In addition to the tree, they brought home spray cans of what they called snow and produced storms and drifts on the inside of our picture window. They drew angels that looked like vampire bats, and after Christmas that stuff wouldn't wash off. Heaven knows we tried, long after the kids had lost interest. By the first of February I was still trying to wash away the remains of what we came to call the ruptured angels. I'd bet a $2 bill that, right now, when the light's just right, I could show you on that glass the outline of those ruptured angels.

That little Yuletide adventure with my kids caused me some temporary embarrassment in the neighborhood. But what I regret about it now is that I didn't get a photograph of that tree in the window, when it was looking its worst.

Such a picture would be a great treasure to me.　　　　　ॐ

Piano Man

During the morning coffee hour at the drugstore the waitress asked if I ever had the yearning to be something other than a newspaper columnist.

Oh goodness yes.

At one time or another I've wanted to be a cowboy, a railroad engineer, a pro baseball player, a highly successful novelist, a geologist, a country storekeeper, a race car driver, a lion tamer, an astronaut, the husband of Elizabeth Taylor when she was 32, a translator fluent in seven tongues, an artist capable of making a living by drawing pictures, and a piano player.

I've lost most of my interest in all the avocations mentioned in the previous paragraph, with the exception of the last three—translator, artist and piano player.

For as long as I've been able to daydream, I've thought it would be wonderful to stand between two people who speak different languages and enable them to understand each other. I can't name a higher calling than that—bringing about understanding between people of separate cultures.

Back in the '50s and '60s I had enough college Spanish left in me to get the smallest taste of how a translator must feel at work. I'm talking about simple matters like helping a tourist, with no Spanish at all, order a meal in a restaurant down in Mexico. Or barter the price of a purse in the market.

But now, since I haven't kept using what little I knew, even that much of my Spanish has faded and disappeared. A shame. I haven't surrendered entirely, though. I bought a new Spanish-English dictionary recently and I've begun doing battle again with all those idioms and those confounded irregular verbs. I may yet be able to state in Spanish something more than, *"El sombrero es en la cama."*

Then about the drawing, which I have given up on. Drawing is such a mystery to me.

I've looked over the shoulder of many artists while their pencils produced casual wavy lines for a minute or two and suddenly, the lines came alive and formed human faces, or wild animals, or birds in flight. Amazing.

Why is it that these people can perform this marvelous trick, and I cannot? How does an artist know, when he quickly makes a few curvy marks on paper, that the lines will magically become a human ear, or a rabbit, or a fine Halloween witch?

This always ticked me off a little. Way back in high school I had classmates who made grades no better than mine, and yet they could draw horses, and soldiers, and you could tell they were horses and soldiers. If I tried to draw a horse, people would ask, "What's that?"

I know, I've been told I could take lessons and learn to draw pretty well. (Maybe not horses, which are hard.) But I never have done it and I don't know why.

It's just like my piano playing, which doesn't exist. I'd forty times rather play a piano than write sentences like this, but I've kept putting off lessons until now I've got these old-age things wrong with my hands and probably it's too late.

Don't worry, I never thought of becoming a concert pianist or anything elevated like that. I'd have been happy playing hymns in church, or good old sing-along tunes in a sedate bar.

I wouldn't need sheet music. I'd play everything by ear, and I'd know a thousand tunes. Customers would walk in the bar and they'd say to newcomers, "See that old dude at the piano? I'll bet you a two-dollar bill he can play any tune you can name, and sing you the words to boot."

Then somebody would come up to the piano and ask, "Can you play *Bicycle Built for Two*?" and I'd say, "Will a bear sleep in the woods?"

And here I'd go, banging out that old melody, and pretty soon all the customers would be up, arm in arm, swaying to the beat and singing it out. "Day-zee … Day-zee … Gim-me your an-swer do …"

I'd be leading the singing and with exactly the right timing I'd yell out, "All right, folks, one more time. All together now …" That sounds like great fun to me.

Wonder what the pay is for that kind of work.   ◌

A Bigger Boy

$\mathcal{S}$everal times a week I drive by an elementary school near where I live. A traffic light stopped me there the other day and I had time to watch a group of children at play.

Maybe a dozen kids were crowded close around a bigger boy, laughing, shouting, tugging at him, competing for his attention. He was head and shoulders taller than the other children. I thought of Mannie, who was one of my first heroes.

I suppose his name was Manuel but I don't remember anything but Mannie. He was Hispanic. I hadn't thought of him in decades, but the tall boy on the school ground brought Mannie's image back to me. I could see his face again, and the way he held himself, and how he walked, so loose and easy.

He was years older than his classmates because his folks were migrant farm workers and they traveled with the harvest. Mannie went with them and would miss at least half the school year. When they returned he would go back into the grade he had not finished when they left, and so he might need two years or more to complete a grade.

Schools used to do that. Students were not promoted just because they were of a certain age. They stayed in the same grade until they passed the work. In those days, that's how the world was.

Mannie was no scholar but in certain areas he was better educated even than our teachers. He was, of course, bilingual. He wasn't entirely fluent in English but he could communicate and he was born speaking Spanish, so I call that bilingual enough. I doubt any teacher in that school was close to fluent in more than one language.

But to me, looking back now, there were far more wonderful things about Mannie. One was that he had no problem whatsoever about going to school with kids so much younger and smaller. He loved us.

When he returned from his travels and showed up at school, we cheered as if a hero had returned in victory. He had seen places we'd only read or heard about. Places our teachers had never seen.

But the best thing about Mannie was his everlasting kindness and helpfulness. He was a gentle giant to us, and he had the kindest face. The smallpox scars on his cheeks seemed to make his smile more gentle.

The smallest children, in the first and second grades, would flock to him on the school ground. He would squat and one would leap on his back and lock arms around his neck. He would scoop two more into his arms. Another might wrap around one of his legs and he would stalk about, like Frankenstein's monster, lugging four little squealing kids.

He was taller than the teacher. If the weather went sour and balky windows needed pulling down, Mannie was up in a second to take care of the problem. If a heavy table needed moving, Mannie would move it. If a child fell at recess and skinned a knee, Mannie was there to pick the kid up.

He was ahead of most of us in arithmetic but weak in reading, and we suffered when Mannie was called on to stand and read because we wanted him to do better than he could. He read with painful slowness and without expression, stopping frequently to puzzle over a word unfamiliar to him.

But then, not ten minutes later, at the request of the teacher he might be standing before us to tell about his travels. Which seemed strange and wonderful. This tall brown boy, who had trouble with our language, knew more about our country than all of us combined.

He had watched whales off the coast of California. Floated without sinking in the Great Salt Lake. Seen trees three times taller than our schoolhouse. Straddled the continental divide.

He had been deep in Mexico and a short way into Canada and through two dozen states and he could talk well about such journeys. We sat still and listened because our friend Mannie was doing the telling. He ought to have been paid as a teacher's helper.

Then one day he wouldn't come to school, and we'd not see him again for another year.   ❧

"You're Fired!"

The other day I had to fill out a form and one of the questions was about employment. The form wanted to know if I have a job.

I said yes, even though some of the customers are always telling me that what I do is not really work.

What interested me the most about the form, it asked me to list jobs I had before the one I have now, and how long I stayed in those jobs, and why I left. I think what they wanted to know is whether I've ever been fired, because being fired is a dark mark on a person's work record.

The directions on the form said if it didn't have enough room for my answers I could attach a sheet of my own. So I attached a sheet before I began. Forms are always asking questions and then not giving you enough blank space to answer. I wonder if the people who design questionnaires have ever been required to fill one out.

Listing my previous jobs, I started out with the one I had the summer of '41, as a tractor hand on the Whitman Ranch outside the town of

Happy, up in the Texas Panhandle. I commented on the attached sheet that this was lonesome work, pulling a plow all day and going to bed at nine o'clock and getting up at four-thirty.

The reason I left that job, one day Mr. Whitman said to me, "I ain't gonna need you anymore." I decided later that I'd been fired.

Also I worked in a drugstore behind the fountain as a soda jerk, or soda skeet as we were sometimes called. I liked this work because I often served girls who drank cherry Cokes that cost a nickel and they stayed in the store looking pretty for an hour or more.

I left that job because the druggist's son came home from college and needed to make some spending money and he took my place. Fired, again.

For ten years I taught school, or tried. I learned a lot more than I taught so I couldn't complain about the pay, which wasn't wonderful. I left that job when the institution I was working for underwent what was called a change of policy, and the new policy didn't require my services. Another way of saying I was fired.

I had a grocery store job for a while in 1938. (I'm not describing these jobs in chronological order, but just when I can think of them.) I sacked potatoes in the back, and threw away the rotten ones. I carried out groceries for nice old ladies who lived four blocks from the store and didn't drive.

The last thing I remember about the grocery job, the manager told me, "I don't need you Saturday. If I need you next week, I'll call you." He has never called.

Here in Houston I got radio work, back in the late '40s and early '50s. I rolled out in the middle of the night and drove to the station in the Lamar Hotel, which has disappeared the same as that job did.

On the radio I gave the weather report and the cattle market and other stuff I thought would be of interest to rural people. I then believed that country folks were the only ones who got up early. I hadn't yet discovered that Houston is loaded with citizens who get out of bed at five o'clock and turn on the radio, not caring anything about the price of

500-pound calves. What they want to know is who won the ballgame while they slept, or what the trout are hitting down in Christmas Bay.

After five years of that nonsense the station manager said to me, "Well, your show just hasn't built." Still another way of saying, "You're fired."

I thought all the way back to the first job I ever had. When I was in second grade I became a magazine salesman. They gave me a neat bag to sling from my shoulder. It contained a dozen copies of the *Saturday Evening Post*. I would walk around and knock on doors and ask, "I don't guess you'd want to buy a magazine, would you?"

The people who answered my knock would agree that they didn't want to buy a magazine, and I never sold one copy. The man who hired me said, "Maybe you're not ready for this kind of work," and he took the bag back. The first time I was ever fired.

I didn't know I'd been fired so many times until I filled out that form.

However, I've never once been fired from a newspaper and that's why I've decided this is a good place to work.   ∾

Message in a Bottle

*M*aybe you saw the story about the ten-year-old boy who released a small helium balloon in St. Paul, Minn. and two months later, a university student in the Czech Republic found the balloon and answered the note the boy had attached to it.

The balloon traveled about 4,500 miles before it was found. I love that story.

Boys of that age have been sending up balloons and throwing sealed bottles into streams for generations, and I doubt they'll ever stop. That sort of dreamy adventure has a universal appeal. I think it springs from the compelling urge to communicate with people beyond the horizon, people who live in different ways than we do.

My sidekick Dude and I were about the same age as the kid in St. Paul when we pitched a pop bottle into the Clear Fork of the Brazos River, up in Shackelford County. Dude's father used to take us fishing on the Clear Fork, on a ranch northwest of Albany, the county seat of Shackelford.

Shackelford County is just north and east of Abilene. The Clear Fork snakes across the northwest corner of that county, through what I once thought was truly wild and lonesome country. It still looks that way on the map but I haven't been there since I was a kid. I'd like to go back but I know I never will, not now.

Dude's father was a fool about river fishing. He'd go even in the middle of winter, and we'd camp out, sleep under old quilts and a tarp on thick beds of dead leaves, and put out throw lines for catfish.

I remember the bottle. It was a Nehi Cream Soda, my favorite flavor. We used it because Nehi bottles were heavy glass and tough and they had long necks that you could seal with cork, whittled to fit, water-tight.

We wrote the note on a sheet out of a Big Chief tablet. We used pencil because Dude decided if we used ink it would blur if the inside of the bottle got wet. I doubt we had a fountain pen, anyway.

I don't remember that we wrote anything dramatic to put in the bottle. At that time, stories about bottles floating in the sea were likely to be about shipwreck survivors. The messages would describe the disasters, and plead for rescue from the desert islands where the survivors were stranded.

Dude and I simply wrote our names and the date and an address and said we were pitching the bottle into the Clear Fork of the Brazos River in Texas and if anybody found the bottle they could write us about where it ended up.

We decided our bottle would travel five miles a day. I don't remember how we arrived at that rate, but we used it to see the thing floating out the mouth of the Clear Fork and into the main stream of the Brazos.

We got a road map and calculated when the bottle bobbed through Waco, and past College Station, and Brenham, and Richmond, and Freeport—all places we'd never been, and didn't expect ever to see.

We saw it riding waves in the Gulf. Then we had arguments about which way it might float. Into the Pacific somehow? To wash up on the beach of a tiny island? To be picked up by a beautiful native girl in a sarong?

No, maybe it would travel across the Atlantic instead, to England or Portugal or Italy or Greece, and it would be found by a genuine European prince, or better yet, a princess.

After a couple of months, without a response, we forgot the bottle.

But sometimes, like when I read about the kid in Minnesota sending up the balloon, I think again about that bottle we pitched in the river so long ago.

The probability is that it hit a rock and smashed, a hundred yards downstream. Or the cork came out and the bottle sank, to live forever on the bottom as a nursery for baby catfish.

Even so.

I still see our bottle lying among the trash somewhere on a lonely beach the other side of the world. Somebody could find it yet.   ∾

Hoop Snake

Recently I was a guest at a polite luncheon down in Lake Jackson, at Riverside Country Club. Attending that affair were lots and lots of women, looking so splendid, dressed in colorful finery to sip their iced tea and eat their lady salads and their chocolate mousse.

After the meeting one of them came up and told me a hoop snake story:

She was at home, and she kept hearing her husband's voice call out to her from a considerable distance, "Open the door! Open the door!"

He sounded desperate so she whipped the back door open to see her husband running full speed toward the house, and in close pursuit of him was a large hoop snake, rolling like a wheel with its tail in its mouth.

The husband did win the race. He flung himself inside and slammed the door and the snake went under the house and was not seen again.

I have heard dozens of hoop snake stories over the past forty years, and that's almost always the way they end, with the snake running under the house.

However, this one at Lake Jackson was unique because I had never before been told a hoop snake story by an attractive woman at a country club luncheon. Usually I hear such stories in icehouses and country post offices and at beer busts and stag barbecues.

In fact, hearing the story at the country club sort of pushed me off track, and I let that woman get away without even thanking her. I didn't get her name, either, or find out exactly where that house is that the serpent ran under, and when that foot race took place. It sounded recent, and that's unusual because most hoop snake stories happened a long time ago.

If you're a new customer here, maybe you don't know about hoop snakes.

I've collected a wagon load of stories about these remarkable reptiles. Herpetologists who know snakes and write scientific books and journals about them say there's no such thing as hoop snakes that do what the stories say they do. Yet I hear people who seem perfectly intelligent saying they've seen hoop snakes rolling across the pasture with their tails in their mouths.

The stories say this snake is far more venomous than any diamondback rattler. It has a stinger on its tail and anything that stinger touches can be sent straight to the undertaker's. Hoop snake can kill a 200-pound man, or a 2,000-pound bull. Hoop snake can sting a giant tree and kill it.

I've been shown 100-foot cottonwoods in East Texas, dead from hoop snake stings. I've had letters from hunters who've shot hoop snakes and seen the stingers on their tails.

No, I've never met a hoop snake but I've been chased by them, two or three times, back when I was just a shirttail kid and believed anything I heard.

We'd be out in the woods and my cousin C.T. would yell, "Look out! Here comes a hoop snake!" And I'd run all the way to the barn without looking back. I wasn't about to lose ground by turning around to see what might be chasing me.

I've talked to snake experts and read the stuff they write and there is, in fact, a reptile called a hoop snake. It's also called a mud snake, and a stinging snake. Scientific name is *Farancia abacura*.

This fellow, according to snake experts, is entirely harmless.

In his book, *Reptiles of North America*, published by Doubleday, Richard Ditmars says the snake often called a hoop or a stinging snake does have a sharp scale at the end of its tail. And when you handle this serpent it tries to poke you with that scale. But it doesn't really sting.

Ditmars also says this snake sometimes lies in the grass in a sort of circle, suggesting a bicycle tire. So maybe that's the source of the popular notion that a hoop snake rolls with its tail in its mouth. The book says it doesn't do any such thing.

I wish I'd had this book back about 1931 when I was running barefooted through rocks and cat claw bushes and prickly pear, to keep those hoop snakes from catching me.　　　　　　　　　　　　ᔆ

Patents Pending

*L*et me invite the attention of inventors, researchers, developers and venture capitalists. I'm about to give away several golden ideas to anybody who wishes to carry them out and make a few million bucks.

This first one has to do with shaving. It's time to liberate the world's men from the chore of lathering their faces and scraping off whiskers. Think of the jillions of hours men spend every day on this planet, standing at bathroom sinks and harvesting stubble.

There's got to be a better way to use all that time and effort. The method of removing whiskers has not really changed since the straight razor came along and put an end to the awful habit of plucking out whiskers one by one.

How about a cream that we could apply to our faces, leave it on about ten seconds, wipe it off, and thus remove the whiskers without damaging the skin? This doesn't seem to me an impossible goal. Any country that can put a toy tractor on Mars ...

Or maybe there's a way to stop whiskers from growing in the first place. I suggest a re-study of what causes men to lose hair on top of their heads, while the hair on their faces is still growing like the front lawn. Then use that data on going bald to develop a product that would have the same effect on a face.

Next, I'm in the market for a kink-proof garden hose and I bet everybody else is too. I've bought six different kinds of hose, looking for one that won't kink. What do I have? Kinks.

Kinky hoses are a hazard to mental health. Say you're busy in the house and you spot one of your favorite plants dying of thirst. You stop what you're doing, go out, turn on a faucet, drag the hose around the house to where the thirsty plant is. Then suddenly nothing but a trickle is coming out of the nozzle because the hose has kinked and you have to go back and find the kink and unkink it. This has got to stop. We deserve kinkless hoses.

An automatic dishwasher that really does wash dirty dishes is a great American need, too. I recently took over the care of the kitchen at our house, for four days a week. This assignment has reminded me of our national automatic dishwasher problem.

During my career as kitchen help in various houses over the last forty years, I have been on a name-calling basis with a dozen different dishwashing machines and I've never found one yet that will wash dirty dishes. If you want clean dishes you have to give them a pretty good washing before they ever go in the machine, which does a good job of rinsing and drying what you've already washed in the sink.

What I want is a washer that will really clean dirty dishes so I won't have to do half the machine's work in advance. This ought to be within the capability of American industry.

Even the U.S. Army had effective dishwashing equipment long ago, during WWII. The first automatic dishwasher I ever saw was at Sheppard Army Air Force Base at Wichita Falls in 1942. It was fourteen feet long and was called a China Clipper. You could put bowls encrusted with the dried remains of GI stew in the Clipper and they would come out the other end of that sucker glistening white, and so hot you couldn't touch them.

Let's go to cars next. I've ridden in these computerized vehicles that are common now. I mean the kind that have a monitor on the dash and the computer alerts the occupants to all manner of developments. Like it flashes that the left rear door is ajar. That an oil change is due at 15,000 miles. Right front tire is five pounds low. Next car payment due August 2nd.

I wouldn't want to drive a car equipped like that. I'm afraid the monitor might flash "Quick! Turn right!" and I'd panic and whip left instead and straddle a fire plug.

But I wouldn't mind having a computer on board that would tell me how far I am from an obstruction when I'm backing up. Like if I'm parallel parking in the dark the monitor could flash, "Hold it, your rear bumper is six inches from the grille of a $50,000 Mercedes."

Now that would be worthwhile, and I don't see why American technology couldn't give us that. Any country that can have a Martian pet rock named Barnacle Bill …

(Author's note: Since I wrote this piece I've been told that this very feature is now available as an option on some of the more pricey cars.) ❧

Many Bears Mountain

The other morning at the supermarket I met a nice lady in canned goods and she wanted to know why I never write anything for little children.

I told her I supposed that very few little children read this column, if any at all, and she said, "Maybe not, but you could write something that parents could read to little children." I said I would think about it.

So I thought about it, and the following is what came forth. (If the regular customers hate it, not to worry, because I don't intend to do this on a regular basis.)

"A Fable for Little Children"

Once upon a time, long, long ago, a little boy lived with his family on the side of a big mountain in a land far, far away. He was called Little Boy.

This great mountain was covered by a dark forest, and it

was known as Many Bears Mountain because lots and lots of bears lived in those woods.

One day Little Boy's mother sent him into the forest and up the side of the mountain to pick berries for breakfast. She said, "Be sure to take your gun, Little Boy, because you might meet a bear."

So Little Boy took his gun and a basket to put the berries in, and he walked a long, long way into the woods where the best berry bushes grew. He picked and picked until his basket was full, and when he started back home he met a bear.

It was not a large bear. In fact, it was just a cub, about the size of Little Boy himself.

"Well, hello there," said the bear. "I am called Small Bear. Who are you?"

"I am called Little Boy," said Little Boy.

The bear came closer, and Little Boy put down his berry basket and raised his gun.

"Is that a real gun?" asked Small Bear.

"Yes, it is," said Little Boy. "I got it for Christmas, and it shoots real bullets."

"Are you going to shoot me?" asked the bear.

"Yes," said Little Boy.

"Why?" asked Small Bear.

"Because," said Little Boy, "if I don't shoot you you'll jump on me and eat me up."

Small Bear laughed. (Bears could laugh in those days.) "I'm just a cub," he said, "and I don't really care anything about eating people. I like berries better."

Little Boy put his gun down. "To tell the truth," he said, "I don't care anything about shooting bears. My father gave me this gun and said it was for shooting bears. My people have always shot bears."

Small Bear nodded and said, "I know the problem. My

family has always eaten people, but I've never seen that it makes much sense. All this killing and eating."

Little Boy then said, "How about a taste of these berries?" He took a double handful from his basket and held them out, and Small Bear ate them eagerly.

"That's a real treat," said Small Bear, licking his hairy lips. "We bears all love berries, but we have to eat them off the bushes one or two at a time. A double handful like this is really wonderful. I didn't nip your fingers there, did I?"

"No problem," said Little Boy. "Have some more berries."

So the bear and the boy spent a long time in the forest, eating berries and talking and becoming friends, and they decided it was foolish for bears and people to keep on eating and shooting one another.

When Little Boy got back home he told about meeting that bear, and what it said about bears eating people and people shooting bears.

But his parents said he couldn't be telling the truth because bears can't talk, and they said if Little Boy didn't quit telling stories like that he'd be going to bed without any supper.

Next day Little Boy went back in the woods and found Small Bear, who had been punished by his parents for telling a story about going into the forest and meeting a boy who could speak bear.

So, for hundreds of years bears kept eating people and people kept shooting bears, and this still goes on in certain parts of the world. Which is a very sad thing because Small Bear and Little Boy were friends from the day they first met and they lived happily ever after on Many Bears Mountain.

The End.

Moral: Reason for the trouble between people and bears, or any other beasts, is nothing but a lack of communication. &

Surviving the Remedy

One of the customers, Dave Durham, says I've been looking a little bilious lately, and recommends I take a dose of calomel.

Durham is joking, or at least I think he is.

But if I did take a calomel pill it wouldn't be my first one. The last one I took was in 1936, or some year close to that, and I hope never again to meet up with anything that's even kin to calomel.

Durham and I are pretty close to the same age, and that's why he's remembering things like biliousness and calomel.

In our growing-up time long ago, bilious spells were common among young people, and calomel was the standard treatment. I don't hear of anybody having bilious spells now but maybe they do and the disease is called by another name.

If you were a country kid in the '30s, now and then your mother would grab your shirt tail and spin you around and hold you by the chin and stare at you and she'd say, "You look bilious."

Then she'd poke calomel pills down your throat and keep you home from school a couple of days.

I just now looked up that word in my dictionary, which says that calomel is a white tasteless compound used as a purgative.

Purgative. Another word I haven't heard in a long time, and I'm not pleased to become reacquainted with it. Few words in our language are uglier.

Something else is, I don't remember calomel being tasteless. A powder form of this medicine was once marketed in what we called papers. You were given a paper of calomel.

Your mother unfolded a small packet and made a little chute of it, and tilted it so the powder spilled into your open mouth. If calomel is really tasteless they must have been adding something to that powder that made it go down your throat like half a pound of rat poison.

After you got it swallowed, everybody in the room sort of backed off, and watched, and waited, to see if you would hold the dose down.

Maybe you weren't really sick, but after you'd taken two or three doses of that calomel powder, I guarantee you'd be sick by then.

In those times a lot of loving mothers, my own included, forced horrible preparations down the throats of their children, trying to keep them healthy. Most of these medicines were purgatives. If you're not familiar with that term, purgative, you can look it up for yourself. I don't want to talk about it.

I can't remember its name, and don't really want to, but I do remember a mixture of herbs that was sometimes given. As a substitute, I think, for calomel. Probably it was cheaper.

Taking that stuff was torture. Your mother applied a spoonful of it inside your lower lip, sort of the way snuff dippers do. But you weren't allowed to spit. You had to hold that evil wad in your mouth until it melted and you swallowed the juice. Ugh. (I hope you're not eating breakfast.)

I'm now convinced, at the time I'm talking about, no medicine taken by mouth was considered effective unless it tasted like seven kinds of horror.

Castor oil, for instance. I always figured if I died and went to hell, castor oil is the only thing the Devil would give me to drink. Except maybe a hooker of Epsom salts as a chaser.

Multitudes of little kids celebrated when preparations like Syrup of Pepsin came on the market, and Milk of Magnesia. Because such medicines, to those children, tasted like dessert after what they'd been getting.

I wonder if Dave Durham, who is the cause of this medicinal outburst, ever suffered from neuralgia.

That's another disease I've not heard about lately and yet in my early times it seemed like half the adults I knew talked about having neuralgia. My dictionary says it's "paroxysmal pain along a nerve." Whatever happened to neuralgia?

Lumbago I don't hear about anymore, either. Or rickets, or gout.

Remember how old Jiggs, in the comic strip Bringing Up Father, suffered from gout and he was always sitting around with one foot in a wrapping the size of a basketball?

You know what my Methodist mother used to say about Jiggs and his gout? Right. She'd say he needed a good dose of calomel.　　　∾

A Sinking Feeling

A fellow called the other morning and offered to sell me a boat. Said it was in first-class condition and had a good price on it.

I told him I wasn't in the market for boats. He asked, "Aren't you the fellow advertised about wantin' a bass boat?" Told him no and he said he had the wrong number and hung up.

He didn't even say he was sorry about disturbing me. I wasn't disturbed much, since I was sitting right here by the phone. But when people dial a wrong number and don't even say they're sorry, I figure they come out of low-grade families who don't practice the basic courtesies.

But that call got me thinking about boats I've known.

Back in my old hometown when we were maybe fourteen or fifteen, my friend Dude and I got to reading Mark Twain's stuff about floating down rivers and we decided to build a raft and do some floating of our own. It sounded like an adventure and that's what we were looking for.

We borrowed a hand saw, without permission, from Dude's dad. We took pocketfuls of nails and hiked out to the city lake and sawed a bunch of willows and scrap lumber and put together this raft. It wasn't a boat, but it was a weak relative of one.

The only trouble with it was that it wouldn't float. Dude made this speech about specific gravity. Much later he became an engineer who traveled over the world and did important things that I never understood but in 1935 he already knew about things like specific gravity, at a time when I didn't dream it had been invented.

Later we found an old heavy wooden boat that was waterlogged and buried in the mud in the upper end of the lake. We dug that sucker out and let it dry in the sun for a couple of weeks. Then in town we collected tar from where the city had filled cracks in the pavement. We melted the tar and patched the leaks in that old boat.

We talked about launching that vessel in the Leon River and paddling it all the way down to the Brazos and into the Gulf of Mexico and then who knows where—maybe south through the Panama Canal and west into the Pacific and where all those beautiful girls were, wearing nothing but grass skirts.

However, I came down with the mumps that year and we didn't go.

After that I didn't have anything to do with boats until they sent me across the Atlantic to attend World War II and the sailors on board said: don't call it a boat because it's a ship. (Unless it's a submarine, and then it's a boat. I still wonder why.)

About twenty years after that conflict was over, when my kids were growing up, I actually bought a boat. We had a shack then, on a lake in Robertson County and we got tired fishing from the bank. So we acquired this boat that was fourteen feet long and green and was powered by a second-hand twelve-horse outboard that would start every second Saturday of almost any month. We had a lot of fun in that old boat, not just fishing but chugging around the lake, waving at neighbors and bouncing off submerged stumps.

After that, I can't remember having any fun aboard a boat, except for the time I went down the Mississippi a little way out of New Orleans on a big paddle wheeler.

But I've done many a day's work on boats. Shrimp boats. Oyster boats. Ferry boats. Barges. Canoes. Speedboats. Party boats. Sight-seeing boats. Bass boats. Sailboats. Fishing boats. Pleasure boats. And I can't remember climbing aboard any such vessel that I wasn't glad when it returned to shore and I could get off.

One time out in the Gulf I stayed fourteen hours on an oceanography research boat, on a choppy day, and I was sick as a yellow dog for twelve of those hours. I told Neptune, the god of the sea, that if he'd just get me back to dry land I'd never again set sail again on his water. And I have not, at least not without asking him to excuse me.

No, I don't want to buy a boat, whether it has a good price on it or not.   ∾

Hot Dates

*W*hen summer gets rolling and the temperature gets up to ninety, I like to make my heat test, to see how it feels to do without air conditioning.

The other day I made a quick trip out of town, just a few hours, but I didn't use AC. A hot day, too. I rolled down the windows in the pickup and drove the way we did before we had cool cars.

It wasn't too bad. I didn't mind the heat as much as the noise, and the smells. You may not remember how much racket you get in an open window when you're running sixty-five or seventy. It's a blast. Drowns out the tunes on the radio. And all manner of evil odors come in.

The main reason I make this test is, I'm curious. I like to remember how things were long ago and often I can't, without finding a way to feel them.

One time for two weeks I drove 3,000 miles up and down and back and forth across the South Texas Brush Country, covering the Great Drought of the '50s. I was driving a '52 Merc. It had no kind of cooler.

That country hadn't had enough rain to settle the dust for more than six years, and the temperature every day was riding above 100. The crows were sitting on fence posts with their tongues hanging out.

I don't want to do that again but I want to remember how it felt, and I can't, not unless I turn off the AC on a hot day. Toward the end of that journey I bought a fifty-pound block of ice and wrapped it in a tow sack and put it on the floorboard of the Merc. Maybe that helped, but I'm not sure now.

Last weekend I spent a couple of nights at the old country house in Washington County, at Winedale. Except for the dog I was alone so I continued my heat test. We do have central air in that old house, and I know we lose a lot of coolness out of the loose windows and the cracks, but the system will keep you from sweating on a hot night.

I didn't turn it on, not once during the weekend.

The daytime temp topped ninety but I sweated it out, and it wasn't so tough. When you're outside and produce some perspiration, you can feel flat cool if you get a little breeze and find a spot of shade. Well, at least you might feel cool for a few minutes.

While cooking in the kitchen I did get uncomfortable. Dog wouldn't stay in there. Went back outside looking for the wind.

I thought about the women who cooked what I ate, back in my early times. A lot of them worked in little old lean-to country kitchens that had to be sweat boxes. Wood or coal-oil stoves surely kept the temperature at suffering highs.

But I don't remember any of them complaining about hot kitchens. They stayed in there and sweated because they had no choice.

I suspect that many of us who live in conditioned air tend to forget that a significant part of the work force still labors out there in the heat. What got me onto this subject today is, I've been watching a roofing crew.

In this high-rise apartment building where we've moved, I can look down on a neighboring house that's getting a new roof. Along about three o'clock the heat on that roof must be withering. Makes me thankful to have a newspaper job.

A multitude of white-haired citizens surely remember high-school dances in sweltering gyms. I'm talking about a time before deodorants.

About 11:30 when the affair was winding down, the girls I danced with gave off a memorable odor. A combination of over-worked perfume, body powder, and sweat. With a tiny hint of rancidity.

To me that was the natural smell of girls, and I loved it.

Only angels know what the boys were smelling like. I'm thankful I didn't have to dance with them.   ∾

What's the Product?

$\mathcal{M}$ ost of us complain about TV commercials, and I've done my share of the complaining.

The ones I truly dislike come in endless bunches every ten minutes when I'm trying to watch a network movie. And they get longer and longer toward the end when I want to get the film over and go to bed. I'm hesitant to start a network movie because I feel like I get more commercials than movie.

However, I have to say that I like certain commercials better than the programs they support.

About a week ago I watched a commercial I thought was the best thing I've seen on TV in a year. I've been watching for it to run again, but if it has I've missed it.

It's about this fellow with a red pickup, and he's fishing in the surf. The truck is backed up to the beach, so it's headed away from the water.

I may have the details wrong because I didn't pay much attention until the guy has this strong strike.

Whatever he hooked is so big he can't reel it in, and he jams the rod into the rear of the truck somehow. I couldn't see how he made that work. Maybe he's got a pipe welded onto the bumper, to stick the butt of the rod in. I don't fish the surf so I don't know any of the tricks.

Anyhow, this huge thing that the guy has hooked is so strong it starts pulling the truck toward the surf. The guy jumps in the pickup and cranks it and guns forward, and still that huge fish threatens to pull the truck into the water.

I can't remember seeing anything on TV that interested me more. What monster of the deep could that fisherman have at the end of his line? I think the phone rang but I didn't move to answer. I stayed glued to the set, to see how this battle ended.

Finally the pickup, being so strong and good, digs into the sand and moves slowly forward and drags the catch onto the beach. But we don't see what the catch is until the excited fisherman comes out of the truck and looks back. He is most amazed when he sees what he has hooked and dragged from the ocean with his red truck.

What it is, it's a submarine.

I don't know how many times that would be entertaining but I loved seeing it once and I'm on the lookout for it again.

However, I'm wondering just how effective that little drama is, as advertising, because I can't tell you right now what brand of truck the fellow had. I was too interested in the adventure to notice.

I do that often. Watch entertaining commercials and when they go off I can't remember what they were meant to advertise.

My favorite commercial of all time was the one about the runaway tire. This was years ago, before color TV. Or at least before color TV at my house.

This tire got loose from wherever it was supposed to be and it started rolling down the side of a mountain. An automobile tire. Not a wheel. Just this tire.

It rolled for miles. It hit bumps and jumped over obstacles. It leaped fences on farms, and hedges. It rolled past country schools and through villages. I never got enough of watching that tire go. I cared about it, and told people to watch for it on TV.

And yet, I can't say now what brand of tire it was.

One day long ago I had lunch with an executive of a rice milling firm. He talked about advertising and he showed me an ad in the day's newspaper. It was an ad bought by his chief competitor, and he was pleased with it.

"This helps my company," he said, tapping the ad of his competitor. "Every time anybody advertises rice, it helps all of us in the rice business."

If that's true, maybe the runaway tire commercial long ago was, in fact, beneficial to all brands of tires. Maybe the people who paid for that pickup commercial, the one that hooked the submarine, maybe it doesn't bother them that I can't remember their brand name.   ❧

3.

The Chamber of Commerce Bull

The Chamber of Commerce bull played the leading role in a livestock improvement program sponsored by the merchants in my little West Texas hometown, back in the 1930s.

Farmers in that region were using poor old bulls on poor old cows, a combination guaranteed to result in poor little calves. Owners of the cows simply couldn't afford to buy decent bulls. So the Chamber of Commerce, always eager to help farmers make more money to spend in town, bought this great bull and made his services available to all. Any livestock owner could bring his cows to visit this bull. The breeding fee was something like a dollar per cow, if it was paid at all.

The Chamber of Commerce bull was kept in a mesquite pasture out north of our little town. He was an ugly, high-headed, red-eyed beast that looked permanently angry. I'm not sure he had much better breeding than our resident bulls, but he sure had them whipped for size.

Driving by his pasture you could often see him standing out on a limestone ridge, his nose to the wind.

"There's the Chamber of Commerce bull," we'd say.

And down at the pool hall the snooker players would make weak jokes about that animal. "If it's ennythang that Chamber of Commerce don't need, it's more bull."

Not all the livestock owners in that territory were farmers. Some lived in town and kept milk cows in the back yard. My family was one of these. Never in all my growing-up time did I go to a party or have a date or attend a football game that I didn't have to milk a condemned cow before I left, and get up early the next morning and do it again.

At a time when I needed the worst way to impress the girls with how sophisticated I was, I was forever being seen leading a milk cow down a city street in search of a vacant lot, where she could be staked out to graze on johnson grass.

Being country then was not cool, folks. Being country even in the *country* wasn't cool. Being country in town was a dark social sin. Everybody in our town was trying to escape the country and get citified. Having a cow in the back yard was a dreadful stigma to me. I wanted to play tennis and get a suntan. Instead I milked cows.

One morning my father said to me, "Pretty soon the cow's gonna come in heat. When she starts bawlin' I want you to take her out yonder to the Chamber of Commerce bull." Then he left town. He was a traveling salesman but he refused to live in a house unless it had a place out back to keep a cow. He loved to be up on Palo Duro Canyon, or on the Colorado River at Marble Falls, thinking about me back home, milking that old cow in the mud.

He had been gone a couple of days when my mother said to me, "The cow is bawling." That was her way of saying that the creature was in heat and needed to be taken to the bull. My Methodist mother did not speak to me of delicate matters like animals being in heat. "The cow is bawling." That said it all.

It hardly needed to be said, since there's nothing in nature less subtle

220

than a Jersey cow in season. She will not sleep. She will not let anyone else sleep. She will climb fences. She will bawl her head off.

It was a Saturday. The worst time. The entire community would be out and about on the streets. The tennis players would be walking up to the park in their white shorts and new sneakers and their smooth suntans. Half of them would be girls, and I was secretly in love with every one, needing so badly to impress them. Some impression. I'm leading a Jersey cow in an embarrassing condition. Bawling every step. Little kids following along, laughing. Dogs running with me, barking.

And the boys among the tennis players giving me a hard time, so the girls could hear. "Hey, how come at ole cow's bawlin' like kat?" They knew very well how come. They'd just lately graduated from milking cows themselves. "Hey, whattza matter with at ole cow? Where you takin' at ole cow?" And then in chorus, as if they'd rehearsed, *"He's takin' her to the Chamber of Commerce bull!"*

It was a long trip across town.

I began to feel better when I finally got to the depot. I had lost the little kids and most of the dogs and traffic had thinned. All I had to do was get the cow across the railroad tracks and over the creek bridge and through the wire gap in the mesquite pasture. Then I could turn her over to the Chamber of Commerce bull and they could go back in the mesquite and consummate their deal in private.

But this was not to be.

When the cow trotted across the bridge, bawling, the bull heard her and answered from up there on his ridge. I had a loose grip on her chain and she suddenly broke free and ran ahead, toward the voice of the master, and I couldn't catch her.

She stopped, and so did I, when we saw that great red monster descending from his hill. Issuing deep, awful bellows. Trotting stiff-legged and high-headed. The Chamber of Commerce bull, advancing to answer the call. A couple of seconds before he came through it, I saw that he wasn't going to stop at the fence. It was a joke of a fence anyhow, three rusty strands of sagging barbed wire. The wires fell away like spider web when that beast trotted through the fence and he came on out to

221

meet our family milk cow on the shoulder of the road, and things were out of my hands.

And so it came to pass, there beside the highway. And I wish I may never again hear music or see wildflowers if half the cars in the county didn't pick that time to file by, while I seemed to be conducting a public cattle breeding demonstration. I believe now it was a funeral procession.

But I'm not certain, because I didn't really look. I went back to the bridge and sat on the rail and faced downstream and pretended I didn't have anything to do with what was going on. I sat there and I made a promise, that if I survived the mortification of that day, I would never again have any close association with bovine creatures. And I have not.

The fruit of that roadside alliance was a useless male calf that my father sold, for two dollars, before it was weaned.

It had the angry red eyes of the Chamber of Commerce bull.   ∾

Radio Religion

During long drives at night I listen a lot to religious programs on the car radio. And I recommend it. You can hear some really remarkable stuff on those shows. Must be hundreds of radio preachers on the air, representing a great range of denominations and styles. Some radio stations often run continuous strings of preachers, one after the other as long as you want to keep tuned. You will hear crying preachers, and drawling preachers, and singing preachers, and shouting preachers, and pleading preachers, and gasping preachers.

When I say gasping, I am speaking of the style of delivery. A gasper will let go of a phrase, and then take a great gasp, and let another phrase out, and gasp again, and so on. The result is something like this: "Now the Lord is up there (gasp), looking down from on high (gasp), and knowing your every pain (gasp), and your every sorrow (gasp), and even if your brother doesn't love you (gasp), even if your *mother* doesn't love you (gasp), the *Lord* loves you (gasp)!"

Some radio preachers have the habit of putting stock religious expressions into everything they say. Expressions like "praise the Lord," and "Lord love you," and "amen," and "glory to God." I get the feeling this habit is so strong on some of them that they don't really know they're putting all those expressions in. Probably it's the same as the speech habits you or I have, such as saying "you know" all the time. A radio preacher with this habit will never say "good evening" to his audience. Instead he will say, "Good evening praise the Lord," and he won't put a comma between the "evening" and the "praise." He'll say it as if it's all one expression.

Once in a while I hear one preacher who gives the two expressions "amen" and "praise the Lord" a thorough working over in his every sentence. I have to admit I'm fascinated by this style, and I look for this gent on the dial when I'm traveling. He will even put in the "amen" and the "praise the Lord" when he's reading scripture, and it gives an exceptional sound to Bible verse you've been familiar with all your life. On the 23rd Psalm, for instance, I think he would sound like this: "The Lord is my shepherd amen; I shall not want praise the Lord. He maketh me to lie down in green pastures praise the Lord. He leadeth me beside the still waters amen. He restoreth my soul praise the Lord …"

I have become a big fan of Sunday morning radio too. You get a good deal of music, and a lot of it is gospel singing and spirituals, and I like those. You are most apt to hear the spirituals early, around eight o'clock. On the early programs you get some interesting announcements, too. Here's one I heard: "And now, our prayers go out to Maples Car Wash." Now what's wrong with that? If a person's gonna pray on the radio, why not for a car wash? Or anyway for the folks who work there, which I guess is what the announcement meant.

One of the principal things I like about Sunday morning religious programs, on the country stations especially, is that I hear so many sounds that remind me of my early churchgoing experiences. For instance, I heard a song leader last Sunday that reminded me of Mr. Weatherly. I am just calling him Mr. Weatherly. I do not remember his name. It might have been Weatherly, but I doubt it.

Anyhow, he was a song leader in the church I was taken to back in my green years. I was fascinated by the style he practiced in leading hymns. Like many song leaders at the start of a verse or a chorus, he would pipe up ahead of the crowd and do a couple of notes solo, to sort of lead off and show the way. Any place in a song that looked like it might need leadership, Mr. Weatherly would let fly his solo notes that way.

The distinction in his style was, on those solo notes, he would inject a jerky sort of *ha* or *he* or *heh* sound into the middle of whatever word he was singing. As an example, say he was leading us into the familiar words, "Praise God from whom all blessings flow." He would get out ahead of us with, "Pray-*haise!* God from whom …" You understand, everybody would join him on the "God," but he would be solo on the "pray-*haise.*" Imagine we were about to sing the line, "Rock of Ages, cleft for me." He would lead away with "Ruh-*hock!* Of ages …" You see how he did? I studied him all the time.

One Christmas he came up to the school to lead carols in a chapel meeting. The first song he chose was that happy one that starts, "Deck the halls with boughs of holly." Of course most of the students had never been to our church. Mr. Weatherly startled them by bulling out ahead with, "Duh-*heck!* the halls with …" Everybody roared with laughter. Mr. Weatherly never did understand why. I felt sorry for him.

On the radio I hear a song leader with a similar style. On that lovely old hymn, "Sweet Hour of Prayer," he led off with "Swuh-*heet!* Hour of prayer …"   ❧

Corn Squeezin's

"I hadn't made any whiskey now in about two years," he said. "but there's still a lot of it made around here in these woods. I've got my riggin', if you want to see that. They tell me the only thing the revenue people will arrest you for is havin' a worm, a copper coil …"

We were way back in the woods of East Texas, never mind exactly where, this moonshiner and me. He said he'd talk about makin' whiskey if I wouldn't put his name in the paper, and we shook on that.

Like every moonshiner I ever met, this one said he no longer makes whiskey, that he just used to make it. Yet he said he now has, on hand, two hundred pounds of sugar. Of course he might be intending to make up a very large batch of cookies, I guess.

"I started it back just after World War II," he said. "Old C----- come and stayed with me one time, fishin', and he drunk so much whiskey he kept us all broke so I told him we'd just *make* some goddang whiskey, and that got me started.

"What you have to do is get you some grain. Wheat, rye, corn. I like rye best. First you wash it, get all the dust out, and pour off that dirty water. Then you have you a container you can put a fire under and cover your grain with clear water and bring it to a boil. Then let it cool and settle out, and add your sugar.

"Put about a pound of sugar to two gallons of water and add your yeast. The way we do it, we'll have two barrels hold about twenty-five pounds of grain in each one and about half a box of this powdered yeast in each barrel, and stir it up good with a boat paddle.

"All right, that's your mash. You let 'er sit about seventy-two hours, or until it quits workin'. When it's workin' it'll bubble and boil, look like a big old fish swimmin' in there. When it stops workin' and all your grain settles to the bottom, you pour off your liquid. What you got there is beer, really. You can drink it, sure. Make you high as a two-tailed cat. But to make whiskey you got to distill it.

"You want to be real careful about what you cook that stuff in. Make it in anything metal, except for stainless steel or copper, you're subject to getting' metal poisoning. Might make you blind, or kill you. Real dangerous. Now some of these fellows around here make it in old fifty-five gallon drums, and go right on. But I wouldn't want to do that …"

I asked if he'd take a drink of moonshine whiskey if he didn't know anything about its source. He said no, he sure wouldn't.

He showed me his whiskey-cooking vessel, a big copper container that tapers toward the top.

"You pour the liquid off your mash into something like this," he said, rapping on the cooper kettle. "You get a fire under it some way, and you cook your fumes off. You have your riggin' with your worm, your copper coil, on top. I rig mine with a glass reflux tube up here, and a thermometer. The reflux tube lets the alcohol vapor go into the worm, and it collects the water and lets it flow back into the barrel. You've got to watch your thermometer. That's the key.

"The idea is, alcohol vapor cooks off a lot sooner than water vapor. Of course water boils at a hundred degrees centigrade, so you don't want your temperature to get over about ninety-five. If it gets over a hundred centigrade then you'll just be boiling water, and you don't want that.

"Your strong alcohol vapors start comin' off at about eighty-seven degrees, and go into your worm. You've got your worm in water to cool it, and you keep the water circulating. So the vapor in the worm condenses and comes out alcohol. That's your stuff, that comes out of the worm. That's your product, right there. They call it white lightning.

"When that son of a gun comes out of there it's about a hundred and eighty proof. It's possible to drink it but it'll take the hide off your mouth. And believe me it's explosive, at that point. Put it in a gasoline engine and it'll run like crazy.

"Now, you need to cut the white lightning back. To do that you use distilled water. Ordinary water won't mix with the alcohol. If you don't have distilled water you can put the alcohol on the stove (very, very carefully) and put plain water in it and bring it to a boil just a second and it'll mix up. But it's better to have distilled water. For one gallon of white lightning you can mix in about half a gallon of distilled and that'll cut 'er down to about ninety-five proof. You can use a little hydrometer to tell what you're doing.

"To make your sure-enough good booze, cut back to about ninety-five proof and buy some of these little wooden kegs, charred inside. They come from Arkansas. I used to get 'em in Houston. Anywhere from ten-gallon kegs down to two. Put your whiskey in there and seal it off and put that son of a gun back for about six months, or as long as you can leave it alone, and you got something better'n you can buy in a liquor store.

"The charcoal takes out the foreign stuff, enzymes they call 'em, and ages your whiskey. Some of 'em put a little lye in it to age it, but charcoal's better. Another way, if you got the right kind of container, is put that charred keg in a barrel of water. You got to seal the keg tight and put a band around it to keep from blowin' the cap. Then just boil the whole keg, and overnight you've aged whiskey ten years.

"That charcoal is where you get the amber color to whiskey. White lightning is clear. And the flavor, it comes from grain. You can make alcohol out of sugar and water and yeast, don't even need the grain. But grain gives you flavor."

I asked where he went to get rye, to make whiskey. The feed store? He frowned. "Well, you got to be careful gettin' it that way. Those feed stores have all got orders. If you buy rye you got to give your name and address and tell what you're gonna do with it. That's how close these revenue people are. Best place to get it is off these old box cars that come through, shippin' grain to Russia."

He talked about costs. Said if he used fifty pounds of grain he'd probably pour fifty-five or sixty gallons of liquid off his mash and distill ten to twelve gallons of alcohol out of that.

"I used to make a gallon of white lightning for two dollars," he said, "but that was before the price of sugar went up. I haven't figured it since then."

Probably it won't surprise you that this fellow doesn't think highly of the law against making whiskey at home. "It's the worst law they ever past," he told me. "Look at all this grain being shipped to foreign countries. Farmers could make alcohol out of it and burn it in their equipment. Of course the women think the men are gonna drink all the alcohol made, and they're against it. But you don't have to make grain alcohol. You can make it out of wood, bark, limbs, almost anything."

You don't have to use fancy equipment, either. "Long time ago these old country folks poured the beer off their mash and cooked it in a pot on the stove and put a cloth over it to catch the fumes. Then they'd squeeze the cloth into a jug, and have alcohol. You've heard of corn squeezin's. That's where it came from."   ∾

Not Quite Kissing

The last few years I have been having trouble with a social custom practiced in this town. Cheeking, is what I call it. A man sees a woman friend he hasn't seen in two or three weeks, he is entitled to put the side of his jaw up against her face, so that for a split second they are in cheek-to-cheek contact.

The instant skin touches skin, both parties make a little smooch sound with their mouths. It's not a kiss. They simply open their mouths a little and then shut them back up, similar to the way fish do all the time.

Most cheeking is done man to woman. What I mean, you don't see many men doing it to other men. Women are often seen cheeking other women but I don't think they enjoy it much.

I don't mean to sound critical of this custom. I fact, I sort of like it but I do think we need some rules set forth. I am fairly new in the field of cheeking and I need guidelines.

For instance, I'd like to know when I am supposed to cheek a lady and when I am not supposed to. Nobody can tell me. So I am just blundering along, writing my own laws of cheeking, based on personal experience and observation.

It's clear that a guy is not entitled to cheek a lady the first time he meets her. Even if he's known her husband forty years, worked in the same office, fought in the same war, he must not cheek her on first meeting.

I don't believe cheeking can properly begin until the fourth meeting. Not even then, unless cheekers have gotten along especially well on the previous three occasions. But that law is underdeveloped. It's been conceived, in my mind, but not really born yet.

Then we have the question of frequency. If a man and a woman meet at the tailor shop and haven't seen one another for three weeks, okay, they can cheek. But if they happen to meet the same afternoon at the grocery store, they mustn't do it again.

Say a man and a woman work together in an office. They mustn't cheek daily. Office cheeking is not proper. However—and this is passing strange—if the two chance to meet in the evening, say at a restaurant, they may cheek freely, even though they have been working side by side all day. It has something to do with the coincidence of the meeting. This rule is still foggy to me.

But what gives me the most trouble is the actual execution of the cheek. I have looked in books on social behavior and I have found no help.

On which side do women wish to be cheeked? There is need for a public understanding on this question, the same as we all understand which side of the street to drive on.

In the beginning I assumed that the thing to do was bear to the right, and aim for contact on the left side of the lady's face.

However, this doesn't always work. I meet women who evidently wish to be cheeked on the right side. Maybe they are left-handed. Others don't seem to prefer one side over the other and this can produce awkwardness. Sometimes you see a couple ducking and dodging and switching directions, looking for an agreement on how to get the maneuver going, and they end up bumping noses and that spoils everything.

This greeting has got to be done with grace or it's not a success.

One thing for certain, a guy must be prepared to change his approach on short notice. Here's an example: You start to do a customary cheek, and you're confronted with a new hair style, one that may hide the entire side of the face that you intended to go for.

To deal with this frustration I use what I call the air cheek, adopted from the basketball term which means the ball was shot and didn't hit the rim, net, or backboard. Doing the air cheek, you don't touch anything. You just lean in and make a quick pass with your jaw and call it a job done.

Women's hats are coming back now and that's another problem. I went up against a new challenge the other day—a friend wearing a hat with a great straw brim that turned sort of down in front. Such hats could destroy the entire cheeking custom.

I saw there wasn't any way for me to work up under that hat and get at her. So I just shook her hand. ∾

Grandma's Gas Well

$\mathcal{D}$id I ever mention to you that I'm an oil heir? Well, I am, and to prove it I've got right here in my greedy hand a check for $18.65.

I get such a check every month and I don't have to do one foreign thing in return for it except sign my name on the back and put it in the bank. Of all the things I have done in this life to make a living, being an oil heir is the easiest. I sure like it.

Furthermore, some months the amount exceeds $18.65. Sometimes the check is $22.17. Other times, it's less than the price of a secondhand shirt, like maybe $7.00.

Would you like to hear how a person gets to be an oil heir?

In my case all I had to do was be kin to Miley Ann Dickerson Hale. She was my father's mother and therefore my grandmother and that's why I get the check. The money comes out of a hole in the ground on Grandma Hale's farm in Erath County. About an hour's drive southwest of Fort Worth.

The oil people set up this rig north of the barn. I know the spot well. I once jammed a mesquite thorn in my foot at that well site. I remember how it felt, and how it took about a month of limping before the soreness went away.

I remember when the leases were being signed, we joked about it. It was a laughable idea that this somewhat pitiless place behind the barn on Grandma Hale's farm would produce anything worth a dollar.

But it did. I was just astonished. They made a well there. A gas well, really, not oil. If any oil is coming out of that hole my palms have not been greased with it. But I don't care to be called a gas heir. I like the sound of oil better.

I suppose you can tell by the size of my check that I am not having any trouble spending all my oil money. This is because there are two kinds of oil heirs and I am the second kind. Too bad.

The first kind doesn't have many kinfolks. So if the oil people come and make a well on their grandmother's old farm, they won't have to split the take with a raft of kin. This is the best kind of oil heir to be.

The reason my check is so small may be traced to the productivity of Grandpa and Grandma Hale. They had nine children and they were bible readers who took seriously the part where the Lord said, "Go forth, and populate the earth." Did they ever populate it. They are one of the reasons baby doctors are now driving around in Porsches and BMWs.

When I heard the oil folks had made a well behind Grandma's barn, I got a numbers guy to explain to me what my interest in all those riches would be. He took a pencil and a piece of paper and spoke as follows:

"First you make yourself a decimal point, see, like this. Be sure you put it way over to the left hand side of the page. Next you start drawing zeros, all in a row to the right of the decimal point. You keep making zeros until you run out of paper and then you pick a number and write it in. Any number you like. It won't make any difference by then. Say seven. Seven's a nice number. So you write a seven and stand back and count the zeros and that's about what your interest in this production is."

Which I thought was not a very nice way to talk about Grandma

234

Hale's Gas Well, which we are all very proud of, despite that we are represented in the enterprise mainly by a string of zeros.

I study this little check for $18.65 and I make a wish. I wish there was a magic way I could have handed $18.65 to the tired-eyed adults who were trying to dig a living out of that old farm in the 1930s. Grandma Hale was gone by then but the land was still in the family. In the Great Depression my own parents retreated to that farm one year, when they could no longer pay rent in town. That old place fed us. Its corn and its black-eyed peas and its milk and butter and eggs fed us, when we couldn't buy groceries at the store.

I think of what that $18.65 would have done then for those struggling folks. That much cash, when a dollar was big as the moon. It might have made the difference between losing the farm and keeping it.

I told that numbers man that this must be a pretty good gas well. Because if I am getting $18.65 a month, with all my zeros, somebody up there close to that decimal point has got to be doing all right. He agreed.

That makes me remember things about the spot where the well is. In my recollection of the time we were all on the farm together, fighting for survival, that place beyond the barn has represented the worst of the scene. It was a poor part of the pasture. It seemed forsaken. Very little grass. Sharp rocks to hurt the feet. Mesquite thorns on fallen twigs. Horned frogs. Red ant beds. Goathead stickers. Lizards hurrying across, looking for shade.

When things died, they were taken to that place to be disposed of in nature's way, and buzzards were often there, either busy or waiting, and so it was not a part of the farm anyone went to by choice.

To me it's become one of the ironies of this life that only a few thousand feet below that ugly crust, a fortune was lying. We were picking our way over it, barefoot, to miss the goatheads and thorns and red ants. We were stepping over all that natural gas down there. The smallest part of it, no matter how far the zeros traveled from the decimal point, would have made us rich instead of poor. ❧

My Friend Munroe

We were the same age, about twelve, when Munroe began coming to our neighborhood several times a week. He came with his mother, who washed and ironed and cleaned house and cooked. Not in my family's house. In another house down the street.

What drew him to our yard was the football. I'd gotten a football for Christmas and he'd wander up and sit at the end of the hedge and watch us play. I wonder now if he'd ever touched a football before then. I doubt it.

But from the first time that ball bounced his way, he could kick and pass and catch it better than any of the others of us. A natural athlete. Tall for his age, maybe a couple of inches taller than I was then, and he had those long muscles that so many good athletes have. I spent two summers trying to do something better, in the matter of sports, than Munroe could. I never did.

This was 1934 and 1935, in West Texas, so all those bizarre rules of racial separation were a part of our social structure. But the rules applied to minors in a strange fashion. They were more complex than the rules governing adults.

For example: Two thirteen-year-old boys, one white and one black, kicking a football in the street wouldn't draw any special notice in our town. But the place where the football was being kicked was significant. The street, that was okay. If they happened to be playing in somebody's yard, that was a little different. It might cause the head of a passerby to turn, see who those boys were, playing together in the yard that way. If the boys went to the playground of the white school to kick the ball, even on a Saturday, that was getting close to a violation. And for a black youngster to play on the white schoolyard when school was going on—well, it just wasn't done.

Munroe and I never talked about the rules but we knew them.

That first winter I had the football, we came close to wearing the thing out in the street. We played a two-man kicking game popular then. You tried to back your opponent to his goal by outkicking him, then to score you had to drop kick over the line.

Drop kicking is almost never seen now but a good drop kicker was held in high regard in the time of Munroe and me. I bet Munroe was the best teen-aged drop kicker in creation. My guess is, though, he never got to play in an organized football game. Too bad.

Munroe did not go into our house, ever. When I would go in for a minute he would say that he'd wait outside.

From Munroe I began to learn a bit, just a suggestion, of what it meant to be black in our town. One day I went with him to the house where his mother was working. We went to the back door. His mother was cooking fried pies. She gave us one and told us to sit on the back steps and eat it and we did.

I knew the family that lived in that house. If I had come to the house alone I would have gone to the front door. If they had given me a fried pie I would have eaten it at the table where the family ate. But since I came with Munroe I went to the back door and sat outside and ate the pie.

I would prefer to remember that I was outraged by this discrimination. But I really wasn't. I mainly felt that it was interesting, to share with Munroe that small black experience. It seemed to me a curious privilege I had as a white—that I could go with Munroe and feel black for a couple of minutes, but he could not go with me and feel white.

Two or three times Munroe took me to his house. It always smelled like turnips cooking. I mentioned that and Munroe said they had been eating lots and lots of turnips lately.

One time I went to a black softball game that Munroe played in. My father took me. He liked going to black affairs because they always seated him on the front row and made him feel special. I was not comfortable on the front row but I didn't say anything to my father because he liked the system. When Munroe came to white softball games he sat down the first-base line, away from the white folks.

The only time I got as angry as I should have gotten was when I visited Munroe's school. It was really bad. It was disgraceful. Even so, I didn't imagine there was anything I could ever do about it. And I was angry only for Munroe, not for the other black kids.

So my awareness of racial injustice was that limited. But it was a beginning, and Munroe was the reason for it.　　　　　ᴏᴡ

Little Emmie

$\mathcal{S}$ometimes I go to a funeral that is not an occasion for mourning but a celebration of a life. I attended one recently up in Brazos County, the funeral of Emmie Pipkin Vick, who was the only mother-in-law I ever had.

She was ninety-seven.

Her grandchildren called her Mimi and many of her relatives and close friends called her Little Emmie because she wasn't quite five feet tall.

I have made a study of Little Emmie's life because I admired the way she lived it.

When she died I hadn't seen her in more than ten years but I kept up with her and toward the end, when she was blind, we swapped a couple of tape letters and I was always inspired by the way her interest in the world never faded.

I believe the last thing she talked to me about as how to cook green beans.

In early summer she would fix snap green beans with new potatoes and there was a trick she had that made this a special treat. I wanted to learn how to fix beans that way but I never found out what the trick was. She said the beans were good because they were fresh out of the garden less than two hours but I think that wasn't the trick. It was something else, secret and mysterious, that was meant to die when she did.

In one of the last letters she also remembered for me the words to an ancient song she sang to my children when they were babies. Song goes:

> Weevilly wheat's no good to eat,
> Neither is your barley.
> Want some flour in half an hour
> To bake a cake for Charley.
> Charley is a fine young lad,
> Charley is a dandy,
> Charley is the very lad
> That stole my striped candy.

Little Emmie had a fine, retentive mind. She could sing songs she hadn't thought of in fifty years. She could quote tons of scripture.

She was one of these rare readers who could consume a newspaper from front to back. She was forever asking me questions about why newspapers do certain things and don't do certain others, and often I wasn't able to answer. Because I just hadn't thought of the questions the way she had.

She taught Sunday school in the Baptist church in Bryan for something like sixty-five years. When she was well into her eighties she was driving a little green Plymouth sedan and she would go around early on Sunday morning and gather up what she called "my old ladies" and take them to church and teach them the Sunday school lesson. Most of her old ladies were younger than she was.

She used to scare me, driving that little green car. She depended on

240

God to lead her around and keep her out of wrecks. I wasn't sure God had time to guide a '52 Plymouth over Brazos County and it made me nervous.

All her children were born in a big white house on College Avenue in Bryan. In the fifties, when traffic on that street began to get heavy, she had a hard time crossing it in that little car. She would wait, and wait, and get tired waiting, and finally she'd say, "Well, Lord, get me across because here I go."

And she'd gun across. Did God guide her? Don't ask me that. All I know is, she drove until she was eighty-five without getting hit.

I knew this woman forty years. Her daughter told me at the funeral that Little Emmie prayed for me every night of every one of those years. Maybe that's why I haven't been clobbered on Loop 610.

Some of my habits didn't quite meet Little Emmie's approval but she never lectured me. And we had our little secrets. I was the only member of the clan who didn't mind being seen walking out of a liquor store, and I'd take Little Emmie a bottle of wine that could last two months. I accused her of drinking it out of her thimble.

I admired most the way she dealt with age. I have tried to take a lesson from her.

She'd say, "I have to keep moving." Here's a person ninety-seven years old and blind and she gave herself assignments. She had a day to dust the house. She'd dust, and rest, and dust some more, and this was an all-day job.

Another day she scrubbed. I am talking about an old blind lady scrubbing her bathroom floor. She could have had it done, sure, but she didn't want to. She wanted to keep stirring. Another day she'd wash. And once every week, her daughter took her to the beauty parlor to get her hair fixed for Sunday. Right up to the last, she seldom missed a service in the church where we all gathered the other day to celebrate her life.

Only a few weeks before the funeral, Little Emmie could tell you the price of gold in London. She could talk to you about windfall profits, illegal aliens, the administration's budget, or nuclear testing. She could talk about Arafat, Khadafy, or Jackie Sherrill.

Even when she was lying up there dying, Little Emmie did a special thing for me. She was surrounded by family members, sitting with her all night, doing everything possible to make her departure smooth.

I found out she didn't have flowers in her room because, being blind, she couldn't see them.

So she saved that, for me. I was allowed to send to her room a great lot of flowers, the only thing she didn't have. She couldn't see them but that was all right. She could smell them, and touch them, and she knew who they came from, and said so.

Which was one of the best things she ever did for me.   ∾

Index

Subject Index